Policy-making and Policy Learning in 14–19 Education

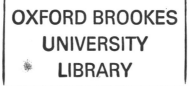

Leading education
and social research
Institute of Education
University of London

Policy-making and Policy Learning in 14–19 Education

Edited by
David Raffe and Ken Spours

Bedford Way Papers

First published in 2007 by the Institute of Education, University of London,
20 Bedford Way, London WC1H 0AL

© Institute of Education, University of London 2007

British Library Cataloguing in Publication Data:
A catalogue record for this publication is available from the British Library

ISBN 0 85473 746 4
978 0 85473 746 8

Typset by www.riverdesign.co.uk
Cover design by Hudson Fuggle
Printed by Elanders Ltd

Contents

List of contributors

Nick Foskett is Professor of Education and Dean of the Faculty of Law, Arts and Social Sciences at the University of Southampton.

John Hart is an independent consultant on education and training policy and an associate of the Centre for Educational Sociology at the University of Edinburgh.

Jeremy Higham is Professor of Post-14 Education Policy and Curriculum in the Post-14 Research Group of the Lifelong Learning Institute, School of Education, University of Leeds.

Ann Hodgson is a reader of education at the Institute of Education, University of London.

Jacky Lumby is a chair of education at the University of Southampton.

David Raffe is Professor of Sociology of Education and Director of Research in the School of Education at the University of Edinburgh.

Ken Spours is a reader of education at the Institute of Education, University of London.

Cathleen Stasz is a senior behavioural scientist at the RAND Corporation and is based at Oxford University.

Ron Tuck is a senior education adviser for Cambridge Education.

Susannah Wright is a research officer, currently working on the Nuffield 14–19 Review of Education and Training, at Oxford University Department of Educational Studies.

David Yeomans is Principal Research Fellow at the Lifelong Learning Institute, School of Education, University of Leeds.

Preface

In an age when governments express their commitment to evidence-informed policy-making a book on policy learning should require little justification. A book on policy learning in the specific area of 14–19 education may require even less justification, particularly for those practitioners and researchers who feel that policy learning has been lacking: that old solutions to 14–19 reform have been repeated and wider opportunities for learning have been ignored.

Several chapters of the book are based on presentations to a seminar at the Nuffield Foundation on 15 March 2005. The seminar was co-organised by the Nuffield Review of 14–19 Education and Training in England and Wales and the Economic and Social Research Council (ESRC) research project on *Education and Youth Transitions in England, Wales and Scotland 1984–2002*, based at the University of Edinburgh. The seminar brought together researchers and policy-makers from England and Scotland to explore how policy learning could benefit from past experience and from 'home international' comparisons of the home countries of the UK.

The 14–19 phase had been on the policy agenda in England and Wales since the late 1980s, so there was an expectation that policy-makers might have learned from experience, notably in the area of vocational education and training which had seen a rapid turnover of policies over the past quarter-century. At the same time, the similarities and differences among the home countries of the UK seemed to offer interesting possibilities for learning. Even if Scotland had no '14–19' policy agenda as such, current curricular, qualifications and institutional policies raised issues similar to those encountered in England and Wales.

A month before the seminar, the Department for Education and Skills (DfES) had published its White Paper on 14–19 education. The immediate context was one of disagreement about the future course of 14–19 education in England, and a sense among many practitioners and researchers that the White Paper reflected a failure of policy learning. This led to criticisms of the style of governance and to accusations of a lack of capacity or will to engage in policy learning in the English system. There was less disagreement about policy directions in 14–19 education in Scotland and Wales, where a more consensual and pragmatic style of governance sought to engage practitioners and researchers in the policy process. Nevertheless there were concerns about both countries' capacity for policy learning and the narrow scope of the learning in which they engaged. And there was a recognition that the home countries could learn from each other, not only from their different styles of governance but also from their different policy directions.

The book may, therefore, have started with a sense of grievance, frustration or impotence. It has ended up with constructive proposals for more effective and inclusive policy-making and policy learning which take account of the complexity of modern governance.

In Chapter 1 we set the scene and introduce the concept of policy learning. We present a conceptual framework that relates modes of policy learning to different models of governance, which we label rationalist, collaborative and politicised. We apply this framework to current policy-making in England, Scotland and Wales. The next four chapters offer different perspectives on policy learning, but they all assess the extent to which policy learning has occurred in practice. In Chapter 2 Jeremy Higham and David Yeomans argue that recent policies for 14–19 education in England reflect policy amnesia, that is, a failure to learn from earlier policy experiences. They base their argument on an analysis of current policies for curriculum flexibility, for vocational diplomas and for employer engagement. In Chapter 3 Ken Spours, Ann Hodgson and David Yeomans examine the Government's attempts to learn from local innovations and best practice partnerships, and demonstrate flaws in its underlying model of learning. In Chapter 4 Jacky Lumby and Nick Foskett suggest that the underlying principles and outputs of 14–19 education have not changed despite the policy dynamism of the past 25 years. They argue that policy learning must be understood in terms of the goals of the learners, that is the policy-makers, rather than in terms of the goals of frustrated advocates of reform. In Chapter 5 John Hart and Ron Tuck describe Scottish reforms from three successive decades: *Action Plan*, *Higher Still* and *A Curriculum for Excellence*. Despite the apparent continuities across these policies the amount of cumulative learning has been limited.

The next three chapters focus on the methodologies of policy learning. In Chapter 6 David Raffe presents a case for home international comparisons and argues that they support a concept of policy learning which is much broader than mere policy borrowing or the identification of good practice. However, the actual influence of home international comparisons is limited. In Chapter 7 Cathleen Stasz and Susannah Wright present a tool for comparative policy learning, in the form of a 'policy instruments and institutions framework' which they apply to 14–19 education policies in the four home countries. In Chapter 8 Ann Hodgson and Ken Spours present a different type of methodology, designed to inform participants in the policy process. They outline an analytical framework based on the concepts of policy eras, the education state, the policy process and political space.

Finally, in Chapter 9 we review the chapters in the book and summarise their concepts of policy learning, their analyses of the current role of policy learning in 14–19 education and their suggestions for improvement. Taken together, the chapters make a case for a more collaborative, inclusive and deliberative mode of policy-making to underpin policy learning: a shift required to address deep-rooted issues in 14–19 education and training in a more complex era of governance.

Acknowledgements

We would like to thank the Nuffield Foundation for hosting the seminar in March 2005, which gave rise to this book and for its commitment to independent research in 14–19 education through the Nuffield 14–19 Review. We are also grateful to the UK Economic and Social Research Council which funded the project on *Education and Youth Transitions in England, Wales and Scotland 1984–2002* (R000239852). The project co-organised the seminar and provided a context for analysing and reflection on differences in policy and practice over time and across the home countries of the UK, and the policy learning that may be based on these. Colleagues in the Centre for Educational Sociology, the Institute of Education and the Nuffield Review team gave valuable help and advice at several stages of the book. They include Delma Byrne, Linda Croxford, Cathy Howieson, Jenny Ozga, Marina Shapira and Marcia Wright.

1 Three models of policy learning and policy-making in 14–19 education

David Raffe and Ken Spours

Introduction

This book asks the question: to what extent can the apparent failures of policy-making in 14–19 education in England, and elsewhere in the UK, be attributed to failures of policy learning? By policy learning we mean the ability of governments, or systems of governance, to inform policy development by drawing lessons from available evidence and experience. Policy learning includes 'experiential learning' from history (Olsen and Peters 1996), learning from other countries (Alexander *et al.* 2000) and learning from local innovations and experiments (Strategy Unit 2003). Effective policy learning increases the effectiveness of the policies that result. In this introductory chapter we first review the evidence that there have been failures of policy learning; we then explore the concept of policy learning in more detail, and discuss three ideal-typical models of the policy process and of the kinds of policy learning which take place within them; finally, we apply these models to 14–19 policy-making in the three home countries of Great Britain.

The apparent failure of policy learning

In 2001–02 the Nuffield Foundation hosted a series of seminars on 14–19 education and training (Nuffield Foundation 2002). The seminars were designed to inform the Foundation's future activities in the area of 14–19 education, and they led to the Nuffield Review of 14–19 Education, launched in 2003. They reviewed different aspects of 14–19 year olds' lives and the education and training opportunities available to them. The seminars concluded with a sense of déjà vu: despite the rapid policy turnover and recurrent institutional restructuring of the previous two decades many of the old problems persisted (Raffe 2002a). They identified a need to learn from this experience and to consider why it had been so difficult to achieve lasting and genuine changes. They also identified a need for the UK systems to learn more from each other.

Over the past quarter of a century, 14–19 education and training in England have been the subject of continuous innovation, but this policy 'busyness' has not always resulted in substantive change (Lumby and Foskett 2005). Each policy innovation, it seems, has failed to learn from the experience of previous innovations; there has been a failure of policy learning. An analysis of 14–19 curriculum initiatives since the 1980s found 'limited evidence for policy learning at the national level' (Higham and Yeomans 2002: 6). Each initiative chose a different model of curriculum change but there was no evidence that its choice was based on systematic evaluation of previous models. In numerous other policy areas, from youth training to vocational qualifications to institutional governance, there has been a continuing cycle of policy innovation with little evidence of cumulative learning. And this inability or unwillingness to learn from the past has been accompanied by superficial learning from the experience of other countries. Throughout the 1980s and 1990s governments borrowed policy ideas from abroad, with little regard to differences of culture or context and with a tendency to borrow from the countries which suited the political mood rather than those which had relevant experience to share (Keep 1991; Finegold *et al.* 1992, 1993). Policy-makers in the four home countries of the UK have acknowledged the potential for policy learning from 'home international' comparisons; but they also accept that such comparisons have had little influence on their policy-making in practice (Raffe 1998; Byrne and Raffe 2005). Despite the rhetoric that devolution would provide a natural laboratory for policy experimentation, the devolved administrations are 'mentally marginalised' in Whitehall; mutual learning is rare and depends on 'accidents of meetings and personal acquaintances' (Parry and MacDougal 2005: 8).

The Scottish Parliament and the Welsh and Northern Irish Assemblies, established in 1999, promised to introduce a more inclusive and deliberative style of governance that would facilitate better policy learning (Paterson 2000a). However, the devolved administrations have had their own apparent failures of policy learning, such as the Scottish 'exams crisis' of 2000. An arrogant and heavy-handed leadership, it is alleged, failed to learn the problems of implementation 'on the ground' and persisted with an over-complex, inappropriately targeted reform, introduced in too much haste with too few resources (Paterson 2000b; Raffe *et al.* 2002). Recent policy forums have revealed dissatisfaction with the limited capacity for innovation in Scottish education and with the failure of policy learning in the face of rapid change and uncertainty (GGIS 2006; Leicester 2006). In Wales, some commentators have criticised the Assembly Government's centralising approach and regretted the absence of a culture of scrutiny (Morgan and Upton 2005). And the devolved administrations' potential for policy learning has been constrained by their limited policy-making capacity, by institutional restructuring and by changes in personnel with the consequent loss of policy memory.

However, the question of policy learning has been raised most acutely in England, where the Government has rejected the Tomlinson Working Group on 14–19 Education's (2004) proposals for a unified curriculum and qualifications framework (DfES 2005), dashing the hopes and expectations of large sections of the 14–19 education community. Where the Working Group had tried to learn from the mistakes of the past, the Government's own proposals seem merely to repeat them. Its plans for specialist diplomas fail to learn the lessons of earlier attempts to develop a vocational track through National Vocational Qualifications (NVQs) and General National Vocational Qualifications (GNVQs) (Raggatt and Williams 1999; Stanton 2004). The proposed general diploma at 16 ignores the lessons of the GCSE, which began by stimulating progression beyond 16 but turned into a barrier for those who did not jump the five A*–C grade hurdle (Hodgson and Spours 2003); the 14–19 White Paper proposes to raise this hurdle. And unlike the Working Group, the Government's own proposals make no attempt to learn from the contrasting approaches to 14–19 learning in Wales and Scotland, or to explain why its own divergent strategy is the only appropriate one for England.

There is, therefore, a prima facie case to answer: that there has been a failure of policy learning in England, and that the issue at least deserves further investigation in Scotland and Wales. In the rest of this introductory chapter we outline a conceptual framework which links policy learning to styles of governance, and we apply this framework to the three home countries of Great Britain.

Policy learning and policy-making: three models

We understand policy learning as an activity of governments or systems of governance. It is more than the sum of learning by individual policy-makers. The fruits of policy learning may be located in the heads of policy-makers, but they may also be found in official records and documents or (more nebulously) in the norms, routines, organisational rules and policy styles of governments (Richardson 1982; March and Olsen 1989). The process of policy learning can be elusive and difficult to study. Many analysts find it easier to study policy learning through its outcomes, and infer that successful learning has taken place if the policies that result are successful (Olsen and Peters 1996). Other analysts associate policy learning with a propensity to innovate (Fullan 1993; Leicester 2006).

4

But the success of policies depends on many other factors than policy learning, and a propensity to innovate may, in fact, reflect policy busyness and the failure of policy learning.

The process of policy learning is therefore social and organisational; it is also political. It would be wrong to see it as a simple rational process based on learning and evidence that is subverted when 'political' considerations are introduced. Policy-making in a democracy is necessarily and legitimately a political process. Olsen and Peters (1996: 33) even suggest that it is a 'mistake . . . to impose norms, procedures, and criteria of relevance from one institutional sphere – science – on another institutional sphere with quite different characteristics – democratic politics'. Political learning is intrinsic to our concept of policy learning, although unlike Olsen and Peters we believe that it should have a social-scientific dimension as well. Political processes may sometimes be in tension with the quality of learning, but they may also be a way to encourage or mediate it. However, we distinguish between the role of politics in policy-making and a 'politicised' policy process in which policy-making becomes centralised, personalised and dominated by ideological or short-term political concerns. We suggest below that a politicised approach to policy-making may produce the worst failures in policy learning.

In this section we identify some theoretical and conceptual tools for analysing policy learning. We draw from a range of relevant literatures, including theories of systems, organisations and institutions; political science, policy analysis and policy science; educational literatures of policy sociology and change management; and analyses of knowledge transfer and research utilisation. These literatures encompass a range of disciplines, methods and research problems. In some of them the concept of policy learning is explicit; elsewhere, as in much of the literature on governance, it is largely implicit. Nevertheless, it is remarkable that analysts and researchers from such diverse starting points tend to converge on a common set of themes and issues relevant to policy learning. We draw some of these themes together into three models of policy-making and policy learning, which we term rationalist, collaborative and politicised (Table 1.1).

In the rationalist model policy learning informs a procedurally rational process of centralised decision-making within a hierarchical system of governance. Power resides with the state, and there is a clear boundary between the public and private spheres. Of the five patterns of governance described by Pierre and Peters (2005), ranging from 'étatisme' to 'governance without government', the rationalist model is nearer the étatiste end of the spectrum. The policy process follows a sequence of distinct and separate stages such as agenda-setting, the determination of policy objectives and priorities, the identification of policy options, the evaluation and selection of options, policy development, policy implementation and evaluation (e.g. Hogwood and Gunn 1984).

Policy learning informs the intermediate stages of this sequence. It is a technical process, separate from the political processes of agenda-setting and the determination of policy objectives and priorities; it is concerned with the choice of means to achieve politically determined goals. It is primarily concerned with knowledge of 'what works', that is, of the most effective policy options in terms of stated criteria of performance. This knowledge is assumed to be transferable: what works within one context is expected to work in other contexts, subject to conditions which must themselves be understood as part of the policy learning process (Rose 1993). These different contexts include different historical periods and different countries: other countries' experiences are trawled for evidence of best practice (Ochs and Phillips 2002). Policy learning may also transfer across policy fields: what works in health policy, for example, may also work in education.

Policy-making in this model is separate from implementation; it takes place at the centre, and results in policies to be implemented elsewhere, but it is informed by the evaluation of policy after

Table 1.1 Three models of the policy process and policy learning

	Rationalist	Collaborative	Politicised
1. Relation of political contestation to policy learning	Separate (concerned respectively with goal-setting and choice of policy options)	Integrated, complementary	Political calculation dominates the policy process causing conflicts and confusions
2. Model of governance	Hierarchical, centralised Policy-making separate from implementation	Collaborative, network-based, decentralised Policy-making close to implementation	Hierarchical, centralised and personalised Political ideology infuses policy-making and implementation
3. Decision-making process	Procedurally rational Distinct stages: e.g. selection of policy goals, choice of policy options; implementation Policy learning informs choice and development of policy options	Deliberative and reflective Stages overlap: political (goals) and technical (options) decisions interconnected; policy development continues in implementation Policy learning informs all stages	Non-rational with tendency for political interventions in policy cycle Stages therefore overlap Policy learning used to legitimise, to gain support for and to implement prior decisions
4. Types of knowledge	'What works' Explicit, declarative, Mode 1 Universalistic; transferable (under discoverable conditions) across time, place and policy fields	Diverse and contested types of knowledge Tacit, procedural, Mode 2, embedded in networks Contextualised; transfer problematic	Diverse types of knowledge politically selected Political learning, legitimating Transferability of ideological paradigm assumed
5. Learning from elsewhere	Used to identify best practice	Used to enhance understanding	Used to legitimate chosen policy
6. Information flows	Knowledge transfer Feedback follows implementation Information gathering through accountability and control mechanisms: vertical information flows	Knowledge exchange Continuous feedback Multiple sources and flows of information: horizontal information flows	Knowledge selection Selective feedback Information gathering through accountability and control mechanisms: vertical information flows Restricted information flows between insiders and outsiders
7. Policy learning relationships	Strongest within policy community; formal relationships with researchers; little continuous practitioner involvement	Developed relationships within policy community and with (and among) practitioners and both established and new research communities	Strong distinction between political insiders and outsiders; extensive use of private research consultants

implementation. This evaluation feeds back into the modification of the policy. The information flows in this model tend to be vertical, between the central government and the various sites of implementation; they are typically structured by procedures for performance management and accountability. The most important policy learning relationships are within the policy community at the centre of the process. Relationships with researchers tend to be formal, contractual and driven by strategic policy agendas; relationships with practitioners tend to exclude or marginalise policy learning.

In the collaborative model governance is less hierarchical and based more on networks and partnership; the boundaries between public and private spheres are weaker. This model is closer to the 'governance without government' end of Pierre and Peters' spectrum. The stages of the policy process are much less distinct (Bowe *et al.* 1992). The distinction between the political process of goal-setting and the technical processes of evaluating options and developing policy is therefore blurred. So is the distinction between policy development and implementation. Policy learning is, therefore, less exclusively concerned with policy development and it is closer both to processes of political contestation and to policy implementation. In contrast to the rationalist model, which separates politics and policy learning, in the collaborative model political contestation is an instrument and a catalyst for policy learning. Policy knowledge is much broader than 'what works', and includes all five types of policy-related knowledge described by Nutley *et al.* (2003): know-about problems, know-what works, know-how to put it into practice, know-who to involve and know-why. Much policy knowledge is tacit, social and embedded in practices and in networks. It is dynamic, uncertain, context-specific and expressed through 'the capacity for practical judgement' rather than formal, propositional knowledge (Hajer and Wagenaar 2003: 24). It resembles the concept of Mode 2 knowledge described by Gibbons *et al.* (1994): trans-disciplinary, contextualised, often tacit, generated in the context of application and socially distributed. Information flows are horizontal as well as vertical: between stakeholders and between different sites of implementation, as well as between the centre and the periphery. They are also more diverse, originating from a wide range of partners, and less structured by accountability and management arrangements. Policy learning relationships with researchers and practitioners are more extensive, more continuous and more diverse than in the rationalist model.

The rationalist and collaborative models are ideal types. Each brings together a number of dimensions that may be more or less closely linked in practice. They are drawn from a diverse range of literatures that, nevertheless, tend to agree that the collaborative model provides the better context for policy learning. This is for two main reasons.

First, the collaborative model more accurately describes actual policy-making processes and the types of knowledge that inform this process. The rationalist model is widely agreed to be a poor representation of how policy decisions are made in practice (Richardson 1982; Olsen and Peters 1996; Smith and May 1997). Similarly, policy-making in practice requires a broader range of knowledge than 'what works', and a model of acquiring that knowledge that is less linear than simple models of knowledge transfer (Nutley 2003).

Second, effective policy learning is more likely to occur in systems of governance characterised by networks, collaboration, weak hierarchy and multiple links between government and civil society, because in such systems there are fewer vertical, lateral and temporal barriers to flows of information (Schon 1971; Bovens *et al.* 2001; Nutley 2003; Hajer and Wagenaar 2003; Pierre and Peters 2005). The weaker boundary between policy decision-making and policy implementation allows the learning acquired during policy implementation to modify and reinterpret policy in the light of local circumstances, and to feed back into central policy-making. Flows of information to policy-makers are more diverse and less distorted by hierarchical relations of management and accountability. Collaborative models facilitate learning and transfer of knowledge that is tacit, context-specific or embedded in networks or in practice. They also allow policy learning to benefit from political contestation, rather than assuming that politics and learning are in tension. Nutley argues that one of the most effective ways in which research knowledge can encourage policy learning is through the process of advocacy, and by being used as ammunition in an adversarial policy-making system. She concludes:

> there may be some benefits from initiatives which seek to introduce more instrumental rationality into the policy-making process but there is even more to be gained from opening up policy-making processes: enabling participation by a wide range of stakeholders and citizens.
>
> (Nutley 2003: 15)

Nevertheless, the collaborative model does not have all the arguments on its side. The rationalist model captures positive features of policy learning which may be absent or less prominent in the collaborative model.

In the first place, the rationalist model draws attention to the methodological issues involved in learning from past experience or from other countries. These issues include the complexity, diversity and dynamism of the policy field, the limited range of policy experiences from which to learn, problems of generalisation and the difficulties of transfer across national, local and historical contexts. They can be obscured by the collaborative model because it focuses on policy learning as the product of relationships rather than as a kind of social science.

Second, the collaborative model may encourage consensual modes of policy-making, which favour single-loop rather than double-loop learning. 'Single-loop learning ... addresses ways of improving the present state of affairs, while double-loop learning brings about a fundamental re-examination of the condition and the current strategies to address it' (Rist 1994: 190). Policy discourses, organisational theories of action and the routines, practices and 'logics of appropriateness' in which they are embedded may filter, interpret and reconstruct information. The effect is to inhibit learning which challenges the assumptions of the discourse itself (Schon 1971; March and Olsen 1989; Ball 1990; Argyris 1999). The rationalist model holds out the promise of more double-loop learning, even if this promise is not always fulfilled in practice.

Third, the rationalist model's notion of stages of the policy process draws attention to the contexts in which different types of policy learning may, or may not, take place. Bowe *et al.* (1992) replace the notion of stages with that of overlapping 'contexts' of education policy-making, which they describe as the contexts of influence, of policy text production and of practice. The willingness of governments to learn, and the types of learning in which they engage, vary across these contexts (Bell and Raffe 1988; Rist 1994). Governments are most likely to resist double-loop learning in the context of practice, when policies are being implemented: such learning directly challenges their legitimacy by questioning the assumptions on which current policy is based. Governments, on the other hand, may be more open to learning in the contexts of influence or of text production and under particular conditions, such as examinations crises, which create conditions for the generation of 'political space' (Hodgson and Spours 2005).

Thus, while the diverse literatures we have drawn on all agree that the collaborative model, on balance, provides the better context for policy learning, some features of the rationalist model may also be desirable. (Critics may argue that these are features of the normative model of rational policy-making rather than of policy-making in practice.) However, actual policy processes may also possess some of the characteristics of a third model, which we term 'politicised'. The politicised model, shown by the right-hand column in Table 1.1, is an ideal type like the two other models although it draws heavily on current observations of New Labour educational policy-making. It could be seen as a distortion of the rational model while, at the same time, including some aspects of the collaborative model, notably through the rhetoric of community and stakeholder involvement.

Whereas politics and policy learning are separate in the rationalist model, and complementary in the collaborative model, in the politicised model they are in conflict because of the propensity of a politicised process to restrict the flow of information and ideas in order to block those which may challenge a preconceived political ideology or project. Policy learning is, therefore, constrained or distorted by its political context. Governance is centralised and hierarchical, as in the rationalist model, but it is dominated by the ideological or political project which may become associated with presidential politics and a dominant personality leading to the marginalisation of sections of the policy-community itself. The project dominates all stages of the policy process, partly because its champions are allowed free rein to intervene in varying contexts; the different stages of the policy process are, therefore, less distinct than in the rationalist model. Policy-making, as a result, is neither procedurally rational as in the rationalist model nor deliberative as in the collaborative model. Policy learning becomes political learning: its main purpose is not to identify policy options and choose among them but to legitimate, gain support for and implement options already chosen by the political project. This can involve utilising diverse types of policy knowledge but the usefulness of knowledge is judged by its compatibility with the project and by its source rather than by the veracity of its evidence. Policy learning relationships reflect a sharp distinction between insiders and outsiders; most researchers and practitioners, and possible many members of the formal policy community itself, are considered outsiders.

As a model of policy learning, the politicised model can reap the worst of both worlds. On the one hand, it lacks the methodological rigour and the capacity for double-loop learning of the rational model; on the other hand, it lacks the rich, continuous multiple information flows of the collaborative model and its ability to use political contestation as a support for learning. There may be a tendency for policy-making processes in either the rationalist or the collaborative model to move towards the politicised model if the government either becomes a prisoner of its own ideology or becomes impatient with the capacity of more consultative processes to achieve substantive change.

Policy-making and policy learning in England

The home education and training systems combine features of all three models but in differing proportions. We suggest that the English education and training system currently experiences a dominance of the politicised model. This can be traced back to the Thatcher years, a period marked by enhanced power for the executive, the growth of alternative sources of policy innovation to challenge the monopoly of the civil service together with new networks of business and right-wing academics formed around neo-liberal think tanks.

In its first Parliament, New Labour's modernisation programme signalled a movement from the ideological politics of Thatcherism towards a rationalist approach that focused on public service concepts of 'best value', 'what works' and how to develop effective policy-making (e.g. Bullock *et al.* 2001; Nutley 2003). This could be seen as part of a broader effort to modernise governance, to promote partnership and public participation in services, to devolve power to regions and nations and to promote joined-up government (Newman 2001).

By 2005, however, New Labour's early reformism had given way to the promotion of competition, diversity and choice in public services. This was the result not only of election manifesto commitments but also of a political agenda concerned principally with retaining the allegiance of sections of the middle classes to state education provision and, more ambitiously, as part of a political project to 're-make' members of the middle classes as 'consumer citizens' in a globalised world (Steinberg and Johnson 2004). This politicisation has also been fuelled by political conflict arising from New Labour's 'legacy politics'. Commenting on the role of Andrew Adonis in the Department for Education and Skills (DfES), the Liberal Democrat education spokesman Ed Davey commented 'The prime minister has had his finger in the pie from the outset [of the Schools White Paper]. Adonis was instructed to deliver something for his legacy' (Glover 2006). Behind the influence of wider politics, the structures of politicisation have also grown. There has been a significantly enhanced role for the Number 10 Policy Unit and other units within government (e.g. the Delivery Unit); an increase in the number of political advisers and political power being openly invested in the hands of a few powerful non-elected individuals, and an increased use of private consultants to carry out the traditional work of civil servants, all of which challenge not only civil servants but also ministers and their departments.

The politicisation of policy has been felt particularly within education because of its totemic significance for the direction of public service reform. However, not all areas of policy may be so vulnerable to this trend. Other less politically sensitive areas may exhibit greater pluralism within New Labour discourse and symptoms of what we have termed a 'collaborative' approach. Certain ministers have argued for strengthening the 'public realm' by promoting more civic involvement and not simply consumer choice (Jowell 2005) as part of the debate about modernising public services through popular involvement in their design and delivery (Leadbeater 2004). Nevertheless, politicised rather than rational or collaborative policy-making appears to be the most influential and its presence can be illustrated through a brief analysis of key tendencies – policy evasion, policy busyness, policy tension, the audit culture and policy amnesia – in 14–19 education.

Politicised policy-making and implications for policy learning

14–19 education is particularly politically sensitive within the overall education agenda because of the role it plays in selection and social segregation (Stanton 2004). These sensitivities focus principally on the role of A level and GCSE qualifications and the role of employers, leading to what can be termed 'policy evasion' and 'no-go areas'. Risk aversion is not a new phenomenon in policy-making (Nutley 2003) but the Government's rejection of the Tomlinson Working Group's proposals for 14–19 reform could be viewed as an extreme case because of the ways in which ministers, following the A level grading crisis of 2002, raised expectations in the education profession and beyond by encouraging 18 months of public debate. Qualifications, however, are not the only sensitive area of 14–19 policy. The role of employers and their contribution to training is another well-known 'no-go' area. Specialist researchers in work-based learning have repeatedly complained of government refusal to consider greater regulation of the youth labour market and more extensive 'licence to practise' – a social partnership model for 'employment' rather than simply policy emphasising the leading role of employers (e.g. Keep 2005). Policy evasion restricts policy learning by not only ruling out certain options but also by not allowing them to be seriously discussed in the first place.

At the same time, politicisation can lead to an irrational policy process which is exemplified by the sheer amount of policy and the rapidity of reform. At the time of writing, English upper-secondary education has had a 14–19 White Paper and its Implementation Plan, the Skills White Paper, the Schools White Paper, the Foster Review of Further Education, the Leitch Review of Skills, QCA's *Framework for Achievement* and the LSC's *Agenda for Change* to name but a few. This 'policy busyness' (Hayward *et al.* 2005) arises from the broader political context – new ministers trying to make their mark and to make the headlines, remediating the impact of previous policy failure and trying to keep to politically determined timetables (e.g. the proposal that all the new specialised diplomas should be rolled out by 2010, a possible election year). This leads to a 'ready, fire, aim' approach in which policy initiatives are rolled out without sufficient evaluation or consideration of implementation issues, amply illustrated by the problematical case of the *Curriculum 2000* reform of A levels, broad vocational qualifications and key skills (Hodgson and Spours 2003).

At the centre of the Government's politicised model is a process of political calculation and triangulation (Toynbee and Walker 2005) as it seeks to maintain middle-class allegiance to state education with the promise of greater school choice or the development of new school sixth forms. This, in turn, produces 'policy tension'. The 14–19 and Education White Papers promote both institutional competition and collaboration (Hodgson *et al.* 2005) with configurations of policy based not on coherent educational concepts or evidence but on a politically inspired mix of public service reform paradigms.

Despite the rhetoric of devolved responsibility to learners and the front line, the mode of governance and the policy process reflect a determined attempt to retain central control (Coffield *et al.* 2005). A key feature of the politicised model of governance is the influence of the 'audit culture' as a particular form of regulation. Originally a part of the Conservative's New Public Management, the audit culture has been amplified by the Government's attempts to justify increased levels of public expenditure (Newman 2001; Steinberg and Johnson 2004) illustrated by the extensive use of policy levers and drivers by the Treasury and various government departments (e.g. targets, inspection and funding regimes). In the field of education, these are exercised primarily through the DfES and its arm's-length agency, the Learning and Skills Council (LSC). One of many problems associated with 'arm's-length' policy levers and drivers is that little is known by policy-makers of their actual effect on professional and institutional practice because the top-down systems created to operationalise them are not designed to encourage feedback.

Within the politicised model, political knowledge is at a premium.

For the Labour Government, this involves applying a general template of public service reform from the health service to other areas of the public sector including education (Strategy Unit 2006). This leads to what could be termed 'lateral insulation' in which 'political' learning focuses on the relationship between different aspects of public service reform. Such a line of analysis suggests that ministers may develop a politicised and general lateral knowledge rather than sharing a deeper and more specific vertical knowledge with researcher and practitioner communities within a given field where 'policy memory' may reside. This form of policy learning begs the question as to whether policy-makers can learn from the past, exercising 'policy memory' and the capacity to reflect upon how policies have fared in different contexts (Higham and Yeomans 2002, 2005).

Constrained learning relationships – practitioners, researchers and policy-makers

Policy learning is based on a variety of policy learning relationships – between policy-makers, practitioners and researchers. Learning relationships within politicised systems, for the reasons already explored, tend to be constrained and hierarchical rather than expansive and open.

Despite its reputation for centralisation England has, in fact, a tradition of bottom-up practitioner innovation in 14–19 education going back to the days of Certificate of Secondary Education (CSE) Mode 3, Technical and Vocational Education Initiative (TVEI) and process-based reform. However, over the last decade this has been increasingly confined to an ameliorating role in making centrally designed qualifications, such as GNVQs or *Curriculum 2000* more workable (Higham and Yeomans 2002; Hodgson and Spours 2003). Practitioners continue to be consulted through Green Papers and important policy initiatives but parameters are restrictive and the timelines for response, short. Practitioner involvement in consultation is also hierarchical. The Government invests a great deal in its relationships with head-teacher and manager groups, selected professional associations and 'elite' selective consultation groups, which integrate chosen practitioners, academics and policy-makers into key policy forums within government.

Despite the drives for centralism and control the politicised approach, however, does not produce a monolithic system. On the ground, there is a flourish of 14–19 innovation by practitioners, assisted by local authorities and local learning and skills councils, around institutional collaboration, developing progression pathways and developing coherent programmes of study (Hayward *et al.* 2005). Local practice takes advantage of the different messages in government policy (e.g. the emphasis on both institutional competition and collaboration) but the question remains as to how far local innovation can be sustained when working against powerful policy steering mechanisms (Hodgson *et al.* 2005).

The relationship between government and the academic education research community in England suffers from an undercurrent of mutual suspicion. The Government has tried to exercise a greater level of control over education research, critical of what it sees as the lack of cumulative research evidence and a lack of engagement with policy needs (e.g. the establishment of the National Education Research Forum (NERF), the funding of a number of 'centres of excellence' and the increasing use of political think tanks and private consultants). Education researchers, on the other hand, have attempted to address government concerns (e.g. Pollard 2005) about the relevance of education research although others have challenged government's 'naïve' belief in 'big science' to provide answers for 'what works' type questions (Furlong 2004). Nutley (2003) argues that the gap between education researchers and policy-makers can only be bridged if each party recognises that it has distinct concerns and problems and both make efforts to develop more mutual understanding.

Within the policy community itself, the Government has

attempted to promote elements of a 'rational' approach to policy-making because of the political priority of encouraging 'joined-up' government (Cabinet Office 1999; CEM 2001). At its most advanced, this approach envisages professionals and policy-makers from different sectors coming together in 'co-configuration' to challenge their own professional traditions and practices in order to find new solutions (Warmington *et al.* 2004). In reality, however, this integrated approach with its demands for more collaborative policy learning has been a relatively minor part of policy-making. The dominant approach, we suggest, has been the broad political application of a public service reform project across different services. Furthermore, the effects of a distinctive English political environment with its top-down governance and policy busyness may undermine attempts at policy learning across different areas of public policy. The sheer number of policy initiatives and short timescales for delivery make it difficult for policy-makers to find time for cross-departmental liaison and evaluation, a situation compounded by reductions in the number of public sector functionaries as a result of the Gershon Review (HMT 2004) together with constant reorganisations both within the DfES and the LSC (Coffield *et al.* 2005).

The various symptoms of politicisation, and the ways in which these support constrained learning relationships, combine together to create a difficult climate for reflective policy learning. Policy evasion, as a resistance to the slow development of necessary long-term measures, goes hand-in-hand with policy busyness and a frenetic pace of piecemeal reform. This results in less time for reflection and works against the idea of feedback from practitioners or researchers. Policy tension and the ensuing political dissension result in political trade-offs and compromises rather than settlements based on policy learning. Policy performativity and the audit culture produce unintended outcomes due to the way they encourage compliance and 'gaming' by different parties within the system (see Lumby and Foskett, Chapter 4 of this volume). Within the politicised policy process, policy learning is not entirely absent but it is dominated by political learning derived from political experience and the need to ensure personal political survival within the higher echelons of government. Learning through rational or collaborative modes is subordinated to these objectives.

Policy learning and policy-making in Scotland and Wales

In Scotland and Wales supporters of political devolution in 1999 hoped to develop a more open and participative style of governance, more consistent with the collaborative model described above (Paterson 2000a; Loughlin and Sykes 2004). Even in Northern Ireland the policy context since the 1998 Good Friday agreement has been defined by aspirations for 'pluralism, democratisation and social inclusion' (Donnelly and Osborne 2005: 149), but with the Northern Ireland Assembly still suspended at the time of writing we focus here on Scotland and Wales.

Many of the institutional forms associated with the politicised model in England, such as central policy units and non-elected advisers detached from policy departments, are absent or weaker in Scotland or Wales. Peter Peacock and Jane Davidson, the respective education ministers at the time of writing, enjoy greater longevity in office and more control over their own departments than any New Labour education minister in England. The scope for presidential or ideological policy-making is restricted by the dynamics of coalition government in Scotland and minority government (since 2003) in Wales. The committees of the Scottish Parliament and Welsh Assembly have potentially more influence than their Westminster counterparts. There is less of the policy busyness found in England: policy-making has been busy but the agendas are less fragmented and less subject to policy tensions. Local government is stronger, and the audit culture is weaker.

In both countries learners, practitioners and other stakeholders have been encouraged to contribute to debates about education policy. In Scotland, the Executive launched a National Debate on school education in 2002, and encouraged wide participation among all stakeholders (Munn *et al.* 2004). This process gave rise, among other things, to the current reform of the 3–18 curriculum, *A Curriculum for Excellence* (SEED 2004). A parallel inquiry into the aims of education was conducted by a committee of the Scottish Parliament, while another committee conducted a wide-ranging review of lifelong learning. In Wales, a similarly wide consultative process led to the *Learning Pathways 14–19* (WAG 2004). More than 170 people from different sectors and stakeholder interests took part in 'Task and Finish Groups', and many others participated in focus groups and other consultation exercises.

In both countries a similar spirit of partnership has informed policy development and implementation (Daugherty 2004). A network model is being used to develop and implement the *Learning Pathways 14–19* in Wales – to the point where a recent report identified a need to rationalise the burgeoning system of partnerships (Chapman 2005). The *Assessment is for Learning* programme (Learning and Teaching Scotland 2005) in Scotland has been seen as an example of a collaborative model of change that has avoided top-down prescription and engaged with the profession (Hayward *et al.* 2004). A similar model is being used for the implementation of *A Curriculum for Excellence*, described by the *Times Educational Supplement* (TES) Scotland as 'a major departure for Scottish education, which in the past has relied on edicts from above rather than organic growth' (TES Scotland Plus 2006: 2). At the time of writing more than 700 schools have joined a register of interest of participants in curricular innovation.

The devolved administrations' commitment to policy learning is also reflected in their engagement with academic research. Historically, links between educational researchers and government have been closer in Scotland and Wales than in England. This partly reflects the smaller scale and denser networks of these countries. Before 1999, it sometimes also reflected an implicit pact between researchers and a territorial leadership asserting its sphere of autonomy within the arrangements for administrative devolution. Since 1999 the devolved administrations have made a conscious attempt to engage researchers. They have also provided active support for capacity building in educational research. The Scottish Executive and Scottish Funding Council have co-funded an Applied Educational Research Scheme with a strong capacity-building remit. In Wales Jane Davidson, the Education Minister, established an Education Research Liaison Group in 2001 in response to reports of weaknesses in research capacity.

The devolved administrations have, therefore, moved some way towards the collaborative model outlined above, and they seem to be much closer to this model than the government in England. Have they, however, solved the problem of policy learning? We suggest three reasons for caution, or at least for suspending judgement on this issue.

The first is that even if Scotland and Wales exemplify the collaborative model they also exemplify some of the potential limitations of that model as a context for policy learning. As we noted earlier, the collaborative model may, under some circumstances, detract from the methodological rigour associated with the rationalist model. It may confuse consultation with research and mistake the strength of consensus for the strength of evidence. It may encourage single-loop learning, which does not challenge this consensus, rather than the double-loop learning, which explores more radical options. Critics in both Scotland and Wales have questioned whether these countries may be developing a consensual but conservative style of policy-making which resists innovation (Reynolds 2002; Martin 2005). It is questionable whether the National Debate in Scotland would have been allowed to engage in the kind of double-loop learning that challenged the assumptions and roles of established policy communities.

Second, the revolution in governance may be incomplete. Welsh critics have noted that old styles of policy-making have persisted and old policy communities have retained their influence, reflected for example in the decisions about the Welsh National Council for Education and Training and the Welsh Baccalaureate (Rees 2002). The decision to reabsorb key educational agencies into the Welsh Assembly Government has been criticised by Morgan and Upton (2005) who argue that the system lacks a culture of scrutiny. Humes (2003) draws attention to aspects of continuity in Scottish policy-making since 1999. And although the Scottish Executive gave verbal support to the Parliamentary Committee investigations on the purpose of education and on lifelong learning, in an apparent spirit of collaboration, it largely ignored their findings in practice. Relations between the research and policy communities have varied, even under devolution: in Scotland there was a period of mutual mistrust under the Executive's first minister of education, Sam Galbraith, a former surgeon whose medical background may have encouraged a narrow understanding of the nature and purposes of educational research. Moreover, to the extent that Scotland and Wales have moved towards a collaborative model this may be temporary, part of a cyclical process linked to the different policy-making contexts outlined by Bowe *et al.* (1992). The commitment to openness has been strong in the context of influence where the administrations have been less committed to particular policy directions and have less to lose by sharing influence. As policies move into the context of policy text production and the context of practice the administrations may become less open to ideas which challenge the wisdom of the chosen policies (Raffe 2002b). A less collaborative and more top-down style may re-emerge. In addition, as we have noted above, either the rationalist model or the collaborative model may evolve into a politicised model if the administration becomes a prisoner of its own ideology or becomes impatient with the pace of change under more consultative arrangements. This could happen in Scotland or Wales as well as in England.

Our third reason for suspending judgement with respect to

Scotland and Wales relates to the discontinuities associated with the devolution process itself. In the short term this process may have reduced the countries' capacity for policy learning by changing the nature of the learning, diverting scarce resources away from policy learning and reducing the stock of policy memory. The new context of political devolution raises questions about the extent to which policy lessons learnt before 1999 can still be applied thereafter. To some extent policy learning may have to begin anew, with a blank sheet. However, the small civil services and small resources for policy-making, already stretched before 1999, now have to accommodate the increased demands of political devolution and accountability. Their capacity for policy learning is tightly stretched. One short-term casualty of devolution, at least in Scotland, was research, which had a low priority in the institutional restructuring after 1999. This was reflected, for example, in a four-year gap between cohorts of the Scottish School Leavers Survey, an important data source for 14–19 education, which had previously contacted new cohorts biennially. Research capacity in Wales is still small in relation to the policy learning needs of a national government (Daugherty 2004). And the organisational changes that accompanied devolution have sometimes resulted in a loss of policy memory. Scottish education policy has become less 'joined up' since the single department of the Scottish Office was replaced by two separate departments of the Executive, one for schools and one for post-school learning. Nearly all the staff of the new Department of Enterprise and Lifelong Learning, responsible for post-school education and training, had to be recruited from other policy areas. As an indirect consequence of devolution the Scottish Inspectorate lost its leading policy-making role, a move which was justified on democratic grounds but which deprived educational policy-making of its main source of policy memory and professional expertise.

Conclusion

We have suggested that policy learning is most likely to take place in systems which have many features of the collaborative model, some features of the rational model and relatively few or weaker features of the politicised model. This optimal balance may be expressed in terms of three types of learning relationships:

- *Learning relationships between government and practitioners* might be marked by the blurring of boundaries between policy-making and implementation; the involvement of practitioners in policy networks; weak hierarchical relationships; established horizontal communications; a supportive accountability framework with information on performance and policy outcomes not distorted by accountability and control mechanisms; and a high degree of sensitivity of policy-makers to issues of deliverability.

- *Learning relationships between government and researchers* are characterised by recognition of the variety of types of 'knowledge' relevant to policy; the involvement of researchers in policy networks and decision-making; mutual understanding and recognition of the different norms of policy and research; government's acceptance of researchers' rights to engage with political debates and a joint commitment to enhancing research capacity to engage in strategic research.

- *Learning relationships within the government/policy community* are marked by a recognition that political contestation can promote learning; a focus on the research and development capacity of government; encouragement and supporting structures for mutual learning across policy fields and sufficient stability of institutions and staffing within government to support policy memory.

In none of the home countries do we find all these conditions. To reach this ideal in England may mean moving away from the politicised model towards a more collaborative style of governance. Scotland and Wales appear to be developing a collaborative model but it remains to be seen whether this will be sustained and, if so, whether it will need to be supplemented by features of the rationalist model.

Acknowledgements

David Raffe's contribution to this chapter was supported by the UK Economic and Social Research Council through the project on *Education and Youth Transitions* (R000239852). We are grateful to Scott Greer, Ann Hodgson and Jenny Ozga for advice and help in the preparation of the chapter. The responsibility for the views expressed in this chapter and for any errors of fact or interpretation is, of course, our own.

References

Alexander, R., Broadfoot, P. and Phillips, D. (eds) (2000) *Learning From Comparing: New directions in comparative educational research. Volume 1.* Wallingford: Symposium.

Argyris, C. (1999) *On Organisational Learning.* Second edition. Oxford: Blackwell.

Ball, S. (1990) *Politics and Policy-making in Education.* London: Routledge.

Bell, C. and Raffe, D. (1988) 'Working together? Research, policy and practice: the experience of the Scottish evaluation of TVEI'. In G. Walford (ed.), *Doing Educational Research.* London: Routledge.

Bovens, M., 't Hart, P. and Peters, B.G. (2001) *Success and Failure in Public Governance: A comparative analysis.* Cheltenham: Edward Elgar.

Bowe, R. and Ball, S. with Gold, A. (1992) *Reforming Education and Changing Schools: Case studies in policy sociology.* London: Routledge.

Bullock, H., Mountford, J. and Stanley, R. (2001) *Better Policy-Making*. London: Centre for Management and Policy Studies, National School of Government, Cabinet Office.

Byrne, D. and Raffe, D. (2005) *Establishing a UK 'Home International' Comparative Research Programme for Post-compulsory Learning*. Learning and Skills Research Centre (LSRC) Report. London: Learning and Skills Development Agency (LSDA).

Cabinet Office (1999) *Modernising Government*. White Paper Cm 4310. London: The Stationery Office.

Centre for Management and Policy Studies (CEM) (2001) *Better Policy Making*. London: CEM, Cabinet Office.

Chapman, C. (2005) *14–19 Learning Pathways in Wales*. Cardiff: Welsh Assembly.

Coffield, F., Steer, R., Hodgson, A., Edward, S. and Finlay, I. (2005) 'A new learning and skills landscape? The central role of the Learning and Skills Council'. *Journal of Education Policy*, 5, 631–56.

Daugherty, R. (2004) 'Reviewing National Curriculum Assessment in Wales: What counts as evidence?'. Assessment Reform Group Symposium, BERA Annual Conference, UMIST Manchester.

Department for Education and Skills (DfES) (2005) *14–19 Education and Skills*. Cm 6476. Norwich: The Stationery Office.

Donnelly, C. and Osborne, R. (2005) 'Devolution, social policy and education: some observations from Northern Ireland'. *Social Policy and Society*, 4 (2), 147–56.

Finegold, D., McFarland, L. and Richardson, W. (eds) (1992, 1993) 'Something borrowed, something blue? A study of the Thatcher government's appropriation of American education policy', Edited special issue containing Parts 1 and 2. *Oxford Studies in Comparative Education*, Part 1, 2 (2), 1–60; and Part 2, 3 (1), 1–128.

Fullan, M. (1993) *Change Forces: Probing the depths of educational reform*. London: Falmer.

Furlong, J. (2004) 'BERA at 30. Have we come of age?' *British Education Research Journal*, 30 (3), 343–58.

Gibbons, M., Limoges, C., Nowotny, H., Schwartzman, S., Scott, P. and Trow, M. (1994) *The New Production of Knowledge: The dynamics of science and research in contemporary societies*. London: Sage.

Glover, J. (2006) 'Red faces in Downing Street'. *Guardian*, 8 February.

Goodison Group in Scotland (GGIS) (2006) *Take Hold of Our Future*. Note of Seminar on 9 March. Godalming: FEdS.

Hajer, M. and Wagenaar, H. (eds) (2003) *Deliberative Policy Analysis: Understanding governance in the network society*. Cambridge: Cambridge University Press.

Hayward, G., Hodgson, A., Johnson, J., Oancea, A., Pring, R., Spours, K., Wilde, S. and Wright, S. (2005) *Nuffield Review of 14–19 Education and Training: Annual Report 2004–05*. Oxford: University of Oxford Department of Educational Studies.

Hayward, L., Priestley, M. and Young, M. (2004) 'Ruffling the calm of the ocean floor: merging practice, policy and research in assessment in Scotland'. *Oxford Review of Education*, 30 (3), 397–415.

Releasing Resources for the Frontline: Independent review of public sector efficiency. London: HMT.

Higham, J. and Yeomans, D. (2002) *Changing the 14–19 School Curriculum in England: Lessons from successive reforms*. Final Report to the Economic and Social Research Council (ESRC). Online. Available HTTP: http://www.regard.ac.uk (accessed 13 September 2006).

— (2005) 'Policy memory and policy amnesia in 14–19 education: learning from the past'. Discussion Paper No. 5, Seminar on Policy Learning in 14–19 Education, 15 March, Nuffield 14–19 Review, OUDES, University of Oxford.

Hodgson, A. and Spours, K. (2003) *Beyond A Levels*. London: Kogan Page.

Hodgson, A. and Spours, K. (2005) '14–19 education and training in England: a historical and system approach to policy analysis'. Discussion Paper No. 8, Seminar on Policy Learning in 14–19 Education, 15 March, Nuffield Foundation. Online. Available HTTP: www.nuffield14-19review.org.uk/files/documents60-1.pdf (accessed 13 September 2006).

Hodgson, A., Spours, K., Coffield, F., Steer, R., Finlay I., Edward, S. and Gregson, M. (2005) *A New Learning and Skills Landscape? The LSC within the learning and skills sector*. Research Report No. 1, TLRP project 'Learning and inclusion within the new Learning and Skills Sector'. Institute of Education, University of London.

Hogwood, B. and Gunn, L. (1984) *Policy Analysis for the Real World*. Oxford: Oxford University Press.

Humes, W. (2003) 'Policy making in Scottish education'. In T. Bryce and W. Humes (eds), *Scottish Education: Second edition post-devolution*. Edinburgh: Edinburgh University Press.

Jowell, T. Rt. Hon. (2005) 'Tackling the "poverty of aspiration" through rebuilding *the Public Realm'*. Essay, 12 April. London: Demos. Online. Available HTTP: http://www.demos.co.uk/catalogue/tessajowell (accessed 13 September 2006).

Keep, E. (1991) '"The grass looked greener": some thoughts on the influence of comparative vocational training research on the UK policy debate'. In P. Ryan (ed.), *International Comparisons of Vocational Education and Training for Intermediate Skills*. London: Falmer.

— (2005) 'Reflections on the curious absence of employers, labour market incentives and labour market regulation in the English 14–19 policy: first signs of a change of direction'. *Journal of Education Policy*, 20 (5), 533–53.

Leadbeater, C. (2004) *Personalisation through Participation: A new script for public services*. London: Demos.

Learning and Teaching Scotland (2005) *Assessment is for Learning*. Online. Available HTTP: http://www.ltscotland.org.uk/assess/for/index.asp (accessed 15 September 2006).

Leicester, C. (2006) *Policy Learning: Can government discover the treasure within?* St Andrews: International Futures Forum.

Loughlin, J. and Sykes, S. (2004) *Devolution and Policy-making in Wales: Restructuring the system and reinforcing identity*. Birmingham: Devolution and Constitutional Change Programme. Online. Available HTTP: http://www.devolution.ac.uk/Briefing_papers.htm (accessed 28 March 2006).

Lumby, J. and Foskett, N. (2005) *14–19 Education: Policy, leadership and learning*. London: Sage.

March, J.G. and Olsen, J.P. (1989) *Rediscovering Institutions: The organisational basis of politics*. New York: Free Press.

Martin, R. (2005) *Public Service Reform in Scotland – The road not taken?* Edinburgh: Centre for Scottish Public Policy.

Morgan, K. and Upton, S. (2005) 'Culling the Quangos: the new governance and public service reform in Wales'. Cardiff: School of City and Regional

Planning, Cardiff University.

Munn, P., Stead, J., McLeod, G., Brown, J., Cowie, M., McCluskey, G., Pirrie, A. and Scott, J. (2004) 'Schools for the 21st century: the national debate on education in Scotland'. *Research Papers in Education*, 19 (4), 433–52.

Newman, J. (2001) *Modernising Governance: New Labour, policy and society.* London: Sage.

Nuffield Foundation (ed.) (2002) *14–19 Education: Papers arising from a seminar series held at the Nuffield Foundation, December 2001–January 2002.* London: Nuffield Foundation.

Nutley, S. (2003) 'Bridging the policy/research divide: reflections and lessons from the UK'. St Andrews: Research Unit for Research Utilisation, University of St Andrews.

Nutley, S., Walter, I. and Davies, H. (2003) 'From knowing to doing'. *Evaluation*, 9 (2), 125–48.

Ochs, K. and Phillips, D. (2002) 'Comparative studies and "cross-national attraction" in education: a typology for the analysis of English interest in educational policy and provision in Germany'. *Oxford Review of Education*, 28 (4), 325–29.

Olsen, J.P. and Peters, B.G. (1996) *Lessons from Experience: Experiential learning in administrative reforms in eight democracies.* Oslo: Scandinavian University Press.

Parry, R. and MacDougal, A. (2005) *Civil Service Reform Post-devolution: The Scottish and Welsh experience.* Birmingham: Devolution and Constitutional Change Programme. Online. Available HTTP: http://www.devolution.ac.uk/Briefing_papers.htm (accessed 28 March 2006).

Paterson, L. (2000a) *Education and the Scottish Parliament.* Edinburgh: Dunedin.

– (2000b) *Crisis in the Classroom.* Edinburgh: Mainstream.

Pierre, J. and Peters, B.G. (2005) *Governing Complex Societies: Trajectories and scenarios.* Basingstoke: Palgrave Macmillan.

Pollard, A. (2005) 'Taking the initiative?'. TLRP and education research. Education Review Guest Lecture, 12 October, School of Education, University of Birmingham.

Raffe, D. (1998) 'Does learning begin at home? The place of "home international" comparisons in UK policy-making'. *Journal of Education Policy*, 13, 591–602.

— (2002a) 'The issues, some reflections, and possible next steps'. In Nuffield Foundation (ed.) *14–19 Education: Papers arising from a seminar series held at the Nuffield Foundation, December 2001–January 2002*. London: Nuffield Foundation.

— (2002b) 'Still working together? Reflections on the interface between policy and research'. In Centre for Research on Lifelong Learning (CRLL) (ed.), *Lifelong Learning, Policy and Research: Rhetoric and reality*. Forum Report No. 9. Glasgow and Stirling: CRLL.

Raffe, D., Howieson, C. and Tinklin, T. (2002) 'The Scottish educational crisis of 2000: an analysis of the policy process of unification'. *Journal of Education Policy*, 17, 167–85.

Raggatt, P. and Williams, S. (1999) *Governments, Markets and Vocational Qualifications: An anatomy of policy*. London: Falmer.

Rees, G. (2002) 'Devolution and the restructuring of post-16 education and training in the UK'. In J. Adams and P. Robinson (eds), *Devolution in Practice: Public policy differences within the UK*. London: Institute of Public Policy Research (IPPR).

Reynolds, D. (2002) 'Developing differently: educational policy in England, Wales, Scotland and Northern Ireland'. In J. Adams and P. Robinson (eds), *Devolution in Practice: Public policy differences within the UK*. London: Institute of Public Policy Research (IPPR).

Richardson, J. (1982) *Policy Styles in Western Europe*. London: George Allen and Unwin.

Rist, R. (1994) 'The preconditions for learning'. In F. Leeuw, R. Rist and R. Sonnichen (eds), *Can Governments Learn? Comparative perspectives on evaluation and organisational learning*. New Brunswick, NJ: Transactional Publishers.

Rose, R. (1993) *Lesson-drawing in Public Policy: A guide to learning across time and space*. Chatham, NJ: Chatham House.

Schon, D. (1971) *Beyond the Stable State*. Harmondsworth: Penguin.

Scottish Executive Education Department (SEED) (2004) *A Curriculum for Excellence. Report by the Curriculum Review Group*. Edinburgh: Scottish Executive.

Smith, G. and May, D. (1997) 'The artificial debate between rationalist and incrementalist models of decision-making'. In M. Hill (ed.), *The Policy Process: A reader*. London: Prentice Hall.

Stanton, G. (2004) 'The organisation of full-time 14–19 provision in the state sector'. Working Paper 13, Nuffield 14–19 Review. Online. Available HTTP: http://www.nuffield14–19review.org.uk/files/documents30-1.pdf (accessed 13 September 2006).

Steinberg, D. and Johnson, R. (2004) 'Introduction'. In R. Johnson and D. Steinberg (eds), *Blairism and the War of Persuasion*. London: Lawrence and Wishart.

Strategy Unit (2003) *Trying It Out – The Role of 'Pilots' in Policy-Making, Report of a Review of Government Pilots*. London: Cabinet Office.

— (2006) *The UK Government's Approach to Public Service Reform – A Discussion Paper*. London: Cabinet Office.

Times Educational Supplement (TES) Scotland Plus (2006), 13 January.

Toynbee, P. and Walker, D. (2005) *Better or Worse? Had Labour delivered?* London: Bloomsbury.

Warmington, P., Daniels, H., Edward, A., Leadbeater, J., Martin, D., Brown, S. and Middleton, D. (2004) 'Learning in and for interagency working; conceptual tensions in joined up practice'. Paper presented at the Teaching and Learning Research Programme of the ESRC (TLRP) Conference, Cardiff, November.

Welsh Assembly Government (WAG) (2004) *Learning Pathways 14–19 Guidance*. Circular 37/2004. Cardiff: Department for Training and Education.

Working Group on 14–19 Reform (2004) *14–19 Curriculum and Qualifications Reform: Final report*. Annersley: DfES Publications.

2   Policy memory and policy amnesia in 14–19 education: learning from the past?

Jeremy Higham and David Yeomans

Introduction

In this chapter we examine three specific examples of recent policies in 14–19 education in England. We suggest that in each of these examples policy-makers could have drawn upon earlier attempts to address cognate issues which thus offered opportunities for policy learning. We find no evidence for such policy learning and argue that consequently key issues associated with the three policies are ignored – indications of what we term policy amnesia. The term policy amnesia seeks to encapsulate dislocations in policy memory despite the fact that the policy problems which are being tackled are often, in broad terms, similar to those which were tackled in the past – and the solutions offered are sometimes not dissimilar to those which have been tried before.

This chapter does not put forward a naïve plea for policy-makers to 'learn from history' in any crude sense, since that notion itself is dubious, given inevitable contextual differences between past and present circumstances. An approach focused upon policy amnesia also risks propagating an individualised, deficit view of policy-makers. In contrast, the argument of the chapter is that there are factors within current policy-making contexts which militate against policy memory and policy learning and which give rise to policy amnesia.

In pursuing this argument, in the second part of the chapter, we draw upon evidence from the broader literature which suggests that policy amnesia and the absence of policy learning is pervasive within policy-making contexts. It appears to exist in a variety of international contexts, across a broad range of social policy fields and within the private sector as well as the public. If this is correct, it follows that the absence of policy learning in 14–19 education in England cannot be explained principally in terms of any particular culpabilities and deficiencies of policy-makers in the field, but must involve some broader sets of factors operating across a wide range of contexts. Explanations might be offered at various levels for this selective, collective loss of memory. We sketch an institutionally based explanation derived from our study of the wider literature to explain the absence of policy-learning in 14–19 policy in England.

In the final part of the chapter we consider the implications of this loss of policy memory and absence of policy learning. Does it matter? If it does, is there anything which can reasonably be done about it or is it naïve to expect an improvement in policy learning, as discussed by David Raffe and Ken Spours in Chapter 9?

Examples of the absence of policy memory in 14–19 reform

In this section we examine three recent policy initiatives and indicate the policy memories which could have been drawn upon in their formulation. These policy memories all derive from policy episodes which are well within the living memories of many current policy-makers and, therefore, would not require extensive knowledge of the history of education or initial delving into archives, but merely an awareness that similar issues and problems to those currently being addressed had been addressed in the recent past and an appreciation that they might yield insights into contemporary policies.

The first example concerns the review *The National Curriculum and its Assessment* by Sir Ron Dearing conducted in 1993 (Dearing 1993) and some of the subsequent policy interventions which have brought about significant changes in the 14–16 curriculum in the ten years which followed the review. The other related examples are taken from the recent White Paper, *14–19 Education and Skills* (DfES 2005a). The first of these concerns the proposal to introduce 14 specialised diplomas in vocational areas during the period 2008 to 2014. The second focuses upon the stated intention that employers should be 'in the driving seat' in the development of these diplomas.

The intention is not to evaluate the policies as such, but to show that in each case they embodied diagnoses of perceived problems and proposed solutions that bore strong similarities to those which had gone before. Furthermore, we shall show that the justifications which were offered included no acknowledgements of earlier reforms and practices and therefore exhibited symptoms of policy amnesia.

The revision of the 14–16 curriculum

The Dearing review was established in a context of growing dissatisfaction with the 1988 National Curriculum and its assessment. Among the issues which Dearing was asked to cover in the review was 'the scope for slimming down the curriculum'. During the process of the review 'the future shape of the curriculum for 14 to 16 year olds' emerged as a particularly significant issue. Dearing stated that schools which allocated 20 per cent of the available time to science and offered full courses in technology and a modern foreign language would have only 15 per cent of the total curriculum time available to provide optional courses. In his report, Dearing rehearsed the various arguments which had been put forward for changes to the 14–16 curriculum. He stated that:

> In the light of consultation I have come to the conclusion that it would be desirable to provide somewhat more scope for schools to build a range of options into the curriculum to complement a statutory core of subjects.
>
> (Dearing 1993: 44)

Dearing provided some suggestions as to how this somewhat greater 'scope' might be used by schools. The essence of these suggestions was that the mandatory elements of the National Curriculum should be reduced. He recommended that history and geography should no longer be compulsory and that technology should not be compulsory in 1994 and 1995. He argued that:

> Schools ought to be able to offer a wider range of choice. By extending the range of options to include courses with a substantial element of applied knowledge and skill – the so-called vocational courses – schools will be better able to provide challenge and motivation across the whole range of student aspirations.
>
> (Dearing 1993: 44)

In the years that followed the Dearing review there were significant changes to the 14–16 curriculum, albeit initially made in a piecemeal fashion, allowing schools to disapply some students from having to study any two subjects drawn from science, a modern foreign language and technology. In September 2004 a more comprehensive reform of the 14–16 curriculum was introduced. English, mathematics, science, information and communications technology, physical education, citizenship, religious education, sex education, careers education and work-related learning were made or remained statutory. The arts, design and technology, the humanities and modern foreign languages became entitlement areas, meaning that they must be offered to students but do not have to be taken.

The overall effect of this decade of change has been to shift from a position in which there was a large statutory curriculum at 14–16 accounting for about 80 per cent of curriculum time for most students towards a curriculum which introduced much more choice, flexibility and differentiation into the curriculum. A particular feature in recent years has been the introduction of much more vocational learning for some students, often conducted in colleges and workplaces, supported by policy initiatives such as the Increased Flexibility Programme (IFP) and 14–19 Pathfinders with associated funding streams and further encouraged by changes in inspection criteria and performance tables.

The policy memory, which might have been drawn upon in relation to these changes, concerned the diverse structure of the 14–16 curriculum before the introduction of the National Curriculum. Benn and Simon (1970), in their study of comprehensive schools, showed how this provided for high degrees of choice, flexibility and differentiation. The options available in one school in the fifth year are reproduced in Table 2.1.

Table 2.1 Subject pools for options in the fifth year in a large 11–18 comprehensive school

1	2	3	4	5
French	History	Geography	Chemistry	Physics
Spanish	Typing	Chemistry	Physics	Biology
History	Technical drawing	Biology	General science	General science
Geography		Typing		
	Metalwork	Scripture	Economics	Art
	Engineering	Art	Social studies	Typing
	Domestic science	Technical drawing	Music	Accounts
	Needlework		Typing	
		Domestic science	Accounts	
	Catering			
	Woodwork	Engineering		

The columns do not include the subjects which all pupils must study: English, mathematics, religious education, careers education and physical education.
Source: Modified from Benn and Simon (1970).

Structuring the curriculum in this way frequently led to high degrees of differentiation by academic ability and gender. Several research studies from this period showed how this differentiation was promoted by formal and informal school processes (e.g. Ball 1981; Burgess 1983). This approach to the 14–16 curriculum provoked considerable criticism in the 1970s and 1980s. Her Majesty's Inspectorate (HMI) described the organisation of options and courses as:

> almost always complex and frequently necessitates compromise on the part of both pupils and schools ... it seems clear that the introduction of options in the fourth and fifth years leads to the abandonment of some important subjects for some pupils and to insufficient breadth in some individual pupils' programmes.
>
> (DES 1979)

In its 1983 statement on the 11–16 curriculum, the Department of Education and Science (DES) stressed the crucial importance of guaranteeing all pupils a curriculum of breadth and depth and which should not be 'over-weighted' in any particular direction. The DES stated that any curriculum which was over-weighted was to be 'seriously questioned' and 'was in direct conflict with the entitlement curriculum envisaged here' (DES 1983: 26).

Partly as a consequence of these sorts of criticisms some schools began to move towards greater commonality in the 14–16 curriculum and in 1988 the National Curriculum introduced a mandatory curriculum occupying around 80 per cent of curriculum time. In turn, a reaction against the comprehensiveness of the National Curriculum has seen the growth of greater differentiation in the 14–16 curriculum. In some schools this has become explicit with the development of particular 'pathways' or 'routes' which students are expected to follow through the 14–19 phase. For example, one school visited as part of the national evaluation of 14–19 Pathfinders (Higham and Yeomans 2006) stated in its Guidance for Choice:

> We currently offer three 'routes' in school which all offer the
> opportunity to follow college courses. The route that you will follow
> will be decided after your interview in school and will be based upon
> prior attainment and assessment criteria.

Route A consisted of an NVQ plus two school option choices; Route
B consisted of vocational science, other vocational GCSEs and other
options; Route C students studied double science, French and three
other options. Three distinct although overlapping routes were thus
identifiable: (1) a route focused on 'traditional' GCSEs including a
modern foreign language; (2) a route focused on vocational GCSEs;
and (3) a route which emphasised NVQs offered at college sites. The
range of subjects offered was similar in some respects to that shown
in Table 2.1, although broadened by opportunities for students to
access courses at local colleges. As in the 1970s, the take-up of
individual subjects, particularly in vocational areas such as beauty
therapy, engineering, hairdressing and painting and decorating was
highly differentiated by gender. This route-based planning of a
differentiated 14–16 curriculum was becoming common in many
partnerships and schools visited during the 14–19 Pathfinder
evaluation.

Thus it is clear that there were strong similarities between the
fundamental assumptions and implicit practices governing the
curriculum in the 1970s school and the 2003 school. However, it
should be acknowledged that the context in which this
differentiated curriculum was developed in the early years of the
current decade was significantly different to that of the 1970s and
1980s. There was sound evidence from our 14–19 Pathfinders
evaluation (Higham *et al.* 2004; Higham and Yeomans 2005, 2006)
and other sources (Golden *et al.* 2005; Ofsted 2005) that the
vocational and other forms of alternative curriculum provision on
offer to 14 to 16 year olds were more systematically planned and
developed, of better quality and offered more secure progression to
further education, training and employment than that provided in

the 1970s and 1980s which was often marked by inadequate planning, variable quality and lack of progression routes. These differences, however, do not negate the significance of policy learning, but emphasise the importance of evidentially and contextually informed comparisons of past and current policy interventions. Any shift in curriculum policy and practice towards greater differentiation also raises fundamental questions about access to areas of knowledge, about the value and meaning of breadth and balance in curriculum, about the balance between choice and compulsion and about the aims and values which inform the curriculum. Evidence that improved alternatives to the traditional, academic curriculum may now be on offer compared to those available 30 years ago may bear upon decisions about differentiation and commonality but do not diminish the enduring significance of questions around the curricular principles referred to above.

At issue in this chapter is not which of the two broad approaches, differentiation or commonality, is better, but whether in the policy-making decision process there was recourse to policy memory and evidence of policy learning. Specifically, in the shift from the high degree of commonality brought about by the National Curriculum to an approach offering much greater choice, flexibility and differentiation there was no evidence that an attempt was made to address the criticisms made of the broadly similar approach in the 1960s and 1970s and show how those criticisms would either be overcome or were no longer relevant or important.

The development of specialised diplomas

Our second and third related examples of policy amnesia are drawn from the recent 14–19 White Paper (DfES 2005a) and the associated implementation plan (DfES 2005b). Having rejected the concept of a unified set of interlocking 14–19 diplomas proposed by the

Tomlinson Report (DfES 2004), the centrepiece of the 14–19 White Paper was the development of 'easily recognisable and understandable Diplomas' which would be available at Levels 1, 2 and 3 in 14 'lines of learning' covering the main occupational sectors of the economy. It was claimed that the diplomas would help to create a more personalised system of learning with 'routes of success for all'. The diplomas will consist of: a core of functional skills in English and maths; specialised learning in the relevant discipline; suitable work experience and any relevant GCSEs or A levels. The process through which the diplomas are to be developed is addressed below when we consider the role allocated to employers.

It should be noted that these are essentially specialised *vocational* diplomas – there are no specialised diplomas in, for example, the sciences, the arts, the humanities or languages. Thus their development must be seen in the context of the White Paper aspiration to strengthen the vocational routes to success. This orientation potentially opens up rich seams of policy memories and policy learning because of the many and varied attempts to achieve similar policy objectives over the last three decades. These attempts go back at least to the publication of *A Basis for Choice* (FEU 1979) which marked the emergence of the new vocationalism (Bates *et al.* 1984) and later saw the introduction of the Technical and Vocational Education Initiative (TVEI) and the formation of the Business and Technician (later Technology) Education Council (BTEC). BTEC subsequently developed a wide range of vocational qualifications of which its First and National diplomas were the most prominent. City and Guilds and the Royal Society of Arts were other awarding bodies who were active in the development of vocational qualifications. Other qualifications developed during the 1980s included the Certificate of Pre-Vocational Education (CPVE) and its successor the Diploma of Vocational Education (DVE). Many of the qualifications achieved some uptake in schools and colleges and the BTEC qualifications remain popular.

From the mid-1980s, and especially after the *Review of Vocational Qualifications in England and Wales* undertaken by the De Ville group (MSC/DES 1986), an attempt was made to rationalise what was seen as the jungle of vocational qualifications. This led to the establishment of National Vocational Qualifications (NVQs), the introduction of General National Vocational Qualifications (GNVQs) and the National Qualifications Framework, which purports to show equivalencies between different types of qualifications.

In the context of this chapter, the aims of GNVQs are particularly relevant. In the 1991 White Paper in which they were introduced it was stated that they would:

- Offer a broad preparation for employment as well as an accepted route to higher level qualifications, including higher education
- Require the demonstration of a range of skills and the application of knowledge and understanding relevant to the related occupations
- Be of equal standing with academic qualifications at the same level

(DES/DOE/Welsh Office 1991: 19)

GNVQs were piloted in 1992 and subsequently became established as significant vocational courses for 14–19 year olds. They were available in a broad range of areas and at Levels 1, 2 and 3 and became a relatively well-recognised route into higher education and to a much more limited extent into employment. GNVQs subsequently underwent considerable change, disappeared at Levels 1 and 2 and were first translated into the Advanced Vocational Certificate in Education (AVCE) and from 2006 into new applied A levels. However, in their earlier manifestations GNVQs embodied some of the apparent features of the proposed specialised diplomas with their focus on breadth, key skills (reformulated as functional skills in the 2005 White Paper) and their pursuit of high status.

This brief review of the very complex attempts to promote vocational education raises questions from a policy learning perspective in relation to the proposed specialised diplomas. Can a high-status vocational route be constructed while maintaining separation from the preserved academic route? Those arguing for a unified system of academic and vocational learning suggest that it cannot – the 14–19 White Paper does not refute this argument or suggest that it is unimportant or over-ridden by other considerations. Policy learning might also have identified a process of 'academic drift' within vocational learning where, in order to achieve 'equal standing', qualifications become more like those with which they seek parity. Again the 14–19 White Paper is silent on this phenomenon – is this to be avoided in the specialist diplomas or to be embraced, as perhaps implied by the suggestion that they should include A levels? The White Paper commitment to 'rationalise the existing very wide array of 3500 vocational qualifications' (DfES 2005a: 47) might be compared with the recommendation from the 1986 *Review of Vocational Qualifications* that there was 'scope for rationalisation' (MSC/DES 1986: 47). However, little rationalisation was subsequently achieved, as shown by the recurrence of the issue almost 20 years later. Various explanations might be offered for this, relating to the interests and values of vocational awarding bodies and the occupational sectors they reflect. It might be argued that the proliferation of vocational qualifications reflects the diversity of commerce and industry in England and is, therefore, functional in terms of the organisation and regulation of training. One person's jungle is another's rich tapestry of flora and fauna. The 14–19 White Paper, however, offers no explanations as to why the rationalisation proposed for the next ten years will succeed where that attempted 20 years ago produced a situation in which there are today 3500 vocational qualifications.

At a more general level the 14–19 White Paper is implicitly strongly critical of earlier attempts to reform vocational education. A policy learning perspective might have led to a questioning of this standpoint. While GNVQs had many critics, they did contribute to gradually improving participation, achievement and progression in post-16 learning in the 1990s. They established a foothold as a progression route into higher education and contributed to progress towards government targets for higher education participation. BTEC diplomas have survived 20 years of upheaval in vocational qualifications and are now attracting rising entries and have credibility with higher education establishments and employers. In the English context, in which vocational knowledge is historically and culturally seen as inferior and in a system in which academic and vocational qualifications are clearly differentiated, it might be argued that these outcomes are not as feeble as implied in the 14–19 White Paper. Policy memories prompt questions as to how, exactly, the new specialised diplomas are going to achieve better outcomes within a broadly similar historical, cultural and curriculum context.

Involvement of employers in the design and development of vocational courses

Our third example of a recent policy which exhibits no evidence of policy memory and policy learning concerns the processes through which the specialised diplomas will be developed and, specifically, the key role assigned to employers within that process. Continuing the theme of the failure of vocational education to meet the needs of employers the White Paper asserted that: 'Vocational education for young people has often failed to command the confidence of employers, higher education and the general public' (DfES 2005a: 20). It also stated that: 'This has been the historic weakness of our education system: not merely that vocational routes are seen by many young people as second class, but also that they are not seen by employers and universities as a sound preparation' (DfES 2005a: 24). This 'historic weakness' is to be overcome by giving employers a key role in the design and development of the new specialised diplomas:

> Crucially, we intend to put employers in the driving seat, so that they will have a key role in determining what the 'lines of learning' should be and in deciding in detail what the Diplomas should contain. That is essential, because these qualifications will only have real value to young people if they are valued by employers. We will therefore put the Sector Skills Councils (SSCs) in the lead.
>
> (DfES 2005a: 47)

In fact, there is a degree of ambiguity within the 14–19 White Paper itself about the role of employers since at other points within the document, higher education and the Qualifications and Curriculum Authority (QCA) appear to have an equal role in development of the diplomas. The conflation of 'employers' with SSCs is also problematic. Keep (2005) comments that it is unclear how much direct consultation there had been with individual SSCs and with individual firms within sectors about their willingness to sign up for this agenda. The *14–19 Education and Skills Implementation Plan* (DfES 2005b) refers to the establishment of Diploma Development Partnerships led by the relevant SSCs which will develop the diplomas.

Policy memory might have led the authors of the 14–19 White Paper to consider a previous attempt to bring about the strengthening of vocational qualifications through an employer-led process. This was the development of NVQs, following the *Review of Vocational Qualifications* (MSC/DES 1986). These qualifications were to be not only employer-led and developed by employers but also largely implemented and assessed by employers in workplaces.

Subsequently, over 1000 NVQs were developed (the National Qualifications Framework database currently lists over 1200 NVQs) and over a period of 15 years many thousands of learners have attained the qualifications. However, detailed studies of the processes by which NVQs were developed showed that this was highly mediated by the Manpower Services Commission (MSC), National Council for Vocational Qualifications (NCVQ) and the industry-led bodies (roughly equivalent to SSCs) (Raggatt and

Williams 1999). The MSC and NCVQ laid down tight criteria for their development specifying that they should be competence-based and that standards should be derived through a process of functional analysis (Bates 1995). Partly because of this, many lead bodies contracted the carrying out of the functional analyses and the actual design of the qualifications to professional training consultants. Thus it is doubtful as to what extent NVQs could be described as employment-led (Field 1995).

The implementation of NVQs has seen wide variations across occupational sectors in their take-up and in the extent to which they have the confidence of employers. Some of the most forceful criticisms of NVQs have come from some employers, while others are much more positive. A detailed study of employers' perspectives on current qualifications in the coloration industry showed that some found lower level NVQs useful (although more for the increased esteem their achievement provided for workers than for increased skills) while the higher level NVQs (Level 3 and above) were seen as much less beneficial (Roberts 2005). Recent research has revealed that 20 years after their introduction there is still limited understanding of NVQs among English employers (Roe *et al.* 2006). Thus the attitude of employers to NVQs has been complex and very variable but despite persistent championing by government and the Confederation of British Industry (CBI) they cannot be said to command widespread confidence (Wolf 2002).

Interestingly, Roberts (2005) also found that employers in the coloration industry were dissatisfied with both the NVQs and the discipline-based qualifications that preceded them and which continued to operate alongside them. However, they had few concrete ideas as to how the situation might be improved or access to mechanisms for doing so. Clearly, it would be illegitimate to generalise from this one case and, indeed, it is a mistake to treat employers as a homogeneous group when considering their contributions to the development of vocational education. However, given the weak commitment to training among many employers, their failure to value vocational qualifications through their recruitment and pay policies and the many other demands on their time from the education system (Keep 2005), their willingness and capacity as a group to take on the role assigned to them in the development of the specialised diplomas must be doubtful.

Thus policy memory deriving from the development of NVQs, and the more general record of employers in developing and supporting vocational qualifications might have given policy-makers cause to pause when placing employers in the 'driving seat' for the design and development of the specialised diplomas. What is to prevent a process of mediation, similar to that experienced by NVQs, involving SSCs, higher education and the QCA through which the diplomas become divorced from employment (although policy memory might suggest that this is highly likely and possibly desirable)? What evidence is there that SSCs have the capacity, skills and willingness to take on the role assigned to them? Evidence from NVQ development was that many lead bodies were unable and/or unwilling to take on their allotted role within the process. A better developed policy memory might have alerted the 14–19 White Paper authors to the fact that involvement of employers in the development of vocational education is neither easy nor a panacea for the production of high quality qualifications which will accurately reflect the needs of employers.

Explanations for policy amnesia

In the previous section, we outlined three recent examples of policy-making in 14–19 which exhibited loss of policy memory and absence of policy learning. Since we have not been inside the policy process our analysis is not, of course, definitive and is based upon public statements and justifications of policy. It is possible that behind the scenes, policy-makers have been deploying policy memory and policy learning but have not wished to display their 'working' publicly (although we can think of no reasons why they should not wish to do so since this would, presumably, strengthen the policy case and pre-empt the sorts of criticisms in this chapter and book). Clearly this opens up research possibilities involving interviews with elite policy-makers designed to probe the presence or absence of policy memory and learning in policy-making processes. The opening of the official archives under the 30 years' rule may also throw further light on this issue.

Based on our current knowledge, however, we suggest that it is unlikely that many policy memories have been drawn upon and much explicit policy learning undertaken. In this section, we offer three closely inter-related explanations for policy amnesia in 14–19 education and training which support this view.

Before turning to the three explanations, it is worth reiterating that our inevitably selective literature review of policy amnesia and the absence of policy learning has suggested that this phenomenon is not restricted to the field of education and training but extends to other social policy fields and into the private sector. There is also evidence that it is at least to some extent an international occurrence having been documented in Holland, the European Commission, the USA, New Zealand and Canada (Pollitt 2000). This raises questions about the levels of any explanations that might be offered. Pollitt suggests that what he calls institutional amnesia may be a manifestation of 'a post-modern focus on an expanded present at the expense of both the past and the long-term future' (Pollitt 2000: 5). In what follows, we eschew such macro-explanations and focus upon the institutional level, although clearly this begs further questions about why a broad range of institutions should experience similar policy memory loss. The broader focus within this section also allows us to reiterate that there is no suggestion that educational policy-makers are peculiarly culpable in their loss of policy memory – rather the suggestion is that they are subject to broader forces or trends which are having effects upon many policy-making contexts.

Restructuring and organisational practices

One possible explanation for policy amnesia concerns the frequent restructuring of policy-making institutions. Such restructuring has been ubiquitous in social policy areas in Britain. The National Health Service (NHS), for example, underwent major restructuring five times between 1982 and 1997–8 (Pollitt 2000; Glennerster 2001). Goodson (2003) shows how the privatisation and restructuring of the British railway industry has brought significant policy memory loss and attrition in professional railway engineering skills. Shaw and Robinson (1998) document difficulties in learning from experience in urban policy.

Educational policy-making institutions have been subject to massive restructuring over the last 15 years. The Department for Education and Science (DES) became the Department for Education (DFE), the Department for Education and Employment (DfEE) then the Department for Education and Skills (DfES); in curriculum and assessment National Curriculum Council (NCC) and Secondary Education Advisory Committee (SEAC) merged to become the Secondary Curriculum Assessment Authority (SCAA) which in turn merged with NCVQ to become QCA; in the development, regulation and funding of further education and work-based learning the Further Education Funding Council (FEFC) and Training and Enterprise Councils (TECs) were first created and then abolished and replaced by the Learning and Skills Council (LSC); youth services and careers services were merged to form Connexions and now face further structural changes following the proposals in the recent Green Paper (DfES 2005c). Each of these changes has brought together institutions with different histories and cultures at times when they were charged with carrying out major reforms within political timescales.

In our second and third examples in the previous section, policy learning may have been particularly strongly affected by the restructuring in the institutions responsible for developing vocational education in England. In particular, the abolition of the Employment Department, the MSC and NCVQ seems likely to have produced a substantial policy memory loss. Institutions designed to help translate employers' requirements into concrete training programmes, from the industrial training boards of the 1960s to the SSCs of the 2000s, have also been subject to regular restructuring, providing little or no institutional continuity.

Nor has restructuring been confined to the external configuration of government departments and agencies. They have also undergone significant internal restructuring and modifications of missions. For example, Hodgson *et al.* (2005) have shown how in its short life, the LSC has already undergone major restructuring and suffered two rounds of substantial job cuts.

This is not to argue that this plethora of restructuring has necessarily brought about significant change. Restructuring may well be an example of what Lumby and Foskett in their chapter (Chapter 4, this volume) call turbulence without change. In relation to schools, Brown (1980) showed how restructuring can often be a substitute for attempting more fundamental change, giving the appearance of reform while achieving limited change to core missions, values and practices. However, in the context of this chapter, restructuring is important because it seems likely to contribute to memory loss both by disrupting historical institutional links and by distracting staff for whom accommodation and adaptation to new structural circumstances will inevitably take precedence over historical policy reflection.

Pollitt (2000) argues that this rash of restructuring within the public sector can be at least partly explained by the importation of what he calls fashionable management approaches from the private sector. At a general level these consist of ideas such as re-engineering, continuous improvement and networking. They involve institutions becoming more fluid, porous and joined-up with flatter, shifting hierarchies. More specifically, they involve much greater use of task-oriented ad hoc groups that form and re-form with shifting memberships to tackle specific policy problems. A related phenomenon is the increasing commissioning of external consultants to analyse policy problems and suggest solutions. We are not suggesting that these sorts of changes have revolutionised institutions, nor that they have brought no benefits, but we do argue that they have contributed to a context in which policy learning is more difficult and policy amnesia more likely.

Mobility of policy-makers

Closely related to the restructuring and changes in organisational practices described above is the institutional mobility of policy-makers. At the political level in education, the last decade or so has seen frequent and rapid changes at Secretary of State level (with the exception of David Blunkett who remained in post for the whole of the first New Labour Parliament). Following Blunkett's move to the Home Office, the Labour Government has reverted to the practice evident under the previous Conservative Government where the Secretary of State for Education and Skills generally remained in office for less than two years. The increasingly high party-political profile of education and training has invested this movement of politicians with more significance than it may have had when the education department was a political backwater. Politicians such as Kenneth Baker, Kenneth Clarke, David Blunkett and Charles Clarke have shown that being Secretary of State for Education can now be a stepping stone to higher office, always provided the office holder can accomplish some highly personal, high profile, innovative and 'successful' policy-making while at education. In relation to the examples in the first part of this chapter it has been shown how Tim Eggar, when a minister in the DFE, provided crucial support for the establishment of GNVQ policy (Sharp 1998; Raggatt and Williams 1999). Following his departure, no succeeding minister was prepared to support GNVQs in the same way and this helps to explain the subsequent transformation and eventual disappearance of the qualification. Also changes in the 14–16 curriculum described in the first part of the chapter cannot be understood without reference to the political and educational difficulties faced by Secretary of State John Patten, which led to his decision to ask Dearing to review the National Curriculum.

The mobility of policy-makers also extends to officials. In his research on senior officials at the European Commission Pollitt discovered that:

> The rule of thumb for ambitious Eurocrats tends to be a move every three years or so, and to acquire a reputation for expertise in depth on a particular topic is as likely to be a barrier to promotion as an assistance. Europe is run by transient generalists.
>
> (Pollitt 2000: 11)

Lingard and Rawolle (2004: 367) state that: 'The on-going restructuring of educational systems, the contractual employment of senior policy officers, the emergence of generic managers, all ensure the loss of policy memory within the processes of educational policy text production.'

The bringing about of this mobility of officials can also be seen as part of a political project to disempower senior civil servants. Certainly the political diaries of Richard Crossman and Tony Benn both attested to the power of senior civil servants in the 1960s, while Margaret Thatcher was later to complain about the inertia imposed upon the DES by its civil servants when she was Secretary of State in the 1970s (Crossman 1979; Benn 1989; Thatcher 1995).

The baleful effect (from the politician's perspective) of the power of senior civil servants was portrayed to satiric good effect in *Yes Minister*. For the politician, the problem with Sir Humphrey Appleby was not a deficit of policy memory, but a surfeit. Margaret Thatcher and Tony Blair have both attempted to change the culture of the civil service with the introduction of appointments from the private sector, the personalisation if not politicisation of civil service appointments, the increasing power and importance of the Downing Street Policy Unit and the large increase in the number of political advisers inside government departments (Kavanagh and Seldon 1989; Rhodes 2001).

Alongside these changes in the civil service there have also been important changes in the relationship between central and local government, with steady attrition in the power of local authorities in education and other social policy areas. In the 1960s and 1970s much, perhaps most, educational policy-making took place within local authorities and Directors of Education such as Clegg, Mason and Tomlinson were important drivers of reform and innovation. The reforms of the last 20 years have meant that local authorities now have much reduced power and capacity to make policy and therefore sources of policy memory and policy learning have been lost. This is particularly significant in relation to the changes in the 14–16 curriculum described in the first part of the chapter since, in the 1960s and 1970s, the DES had limited curriculum knowledge and therefore restricted policy memory. Where such knowledge and memory existed at that time it was mainly lodged at the local level.

Changes in the size and functions of HMI are also likely to have been significant here. Dunford (1998) argues that with the formation of the Office for Standards in Education (Ofsted) in 1992, the reduction in the number of HMIs and their change in primary role from inspection to the regulation of other inspectors, there was a shift in their focus from a national view to the monitoring of individual institutions. Thus the conditions which led to the type of HMI commentary which contributed to the move away from strongly differentiated curricula in the 1970s and 1980s are not present in the same way in the current decade. Nor is the inspection context, with its focus on performativity and the performance of individual institutions, susceptible to the dredging up of policy memories from that period.

Emphasis upon innovation in policy-making

The third factor leading to policy memory loss is the emphasis upon innovation in policy-making. This has been a feature of policy-making for several years and has been reinforced under New Labour. This was illustrated by the leaked 2000 memo from Tony Blair to Alistair Campbell in which he called for an eye-catching initiative in relation to crime, 'something tough, with immediate bite which sends a message through the system' (quoted in Cohen 2003). This approach to policy-making bears strongly upon the assumptive and normative worlds in which policy-makers operate. Pollitt refers to:

> The popularity of ideas of unceasing, radical change. These include some of the most fashionable improvement techniques in the public sector, such as re-engineering and benchmarking. These systems of ideas include suggestions that the past is no longer relevant, or even that to look back is defeatist and dangerous.
>
> (Pollitt 2000: 8)

He returns to his theme of the importation of ideas and concepts from the private into the public sector by arguing that approaches such as re-engineering and continuous improvement have leached from the corporate sector into the public sector. He states: 'a whole (management) industry has grown up implicitly founded on the assumption that what is past is largely irrelevant and what is important to know is what is (allegedly) new' (Pollitt 2000: 12).

These quotations sum up well a policy discourse in which the emphasis is upon the new, the radical, the innovative. The *14–19 Education and Skills* White Paper, for example, states that: 'We propose therefore a radical reform of the system of 14–19 education – curriculum, assessment and the range of opportunities on offer' (DfES 2005a: 4) and 'The system for 14–19 education – curriculum, assessment and the range of opportunities on offer – needs radical modernisation to meet contemporary and future demands' (DfES 2005a: 10).

The reality of policy change may be rather different, since as we illustrated in the first part of this chapter, neither the problems that are being addressed nor the solutions being offered are necessarily new, radical or innovative. The 14–19 White Paper is a good illustration of this as shown by the examples outlined in the first part of the chapter. 'Tinkering towards utopia' (Tyack and Cuban 1995) may be a perfectly defensible approach to policy change but is not to be admitted to within a discourse in which there is a premium on 'eye-catching initiatives'.

In explaining this, Lingard and Rawolle (2004), in their study of the influence of the media on education policy, drew on Bourdieu's concept of 'permanent amnesia'. Bourdieu developed this through his study of the media and referred to: 'the ways in which the media report some issues without any recourse to earlier events or even earlier stories, unlike modernist social science where there is an imperative to build on what has gone before' (Lingard and Rawolle 2004: 367).

The contrast drawn between the media and 'modernist social science' recalls Pollitt's suggestion that the loss of policy memory might be part of a broader post-modernist shift. Bourdieu refers to permanent amnesia as part of the logic of the practice of journalism but Lingard and Rawolle suggest that: 'the concept of permanent amnesia has some purchase as a descriptor for aspects of the logic of practice in the sub-field of educational policy in respect of policy text formation' (Lingard and Rawolle 2004: 367).

They further suggest that this may be an example of a cross-field effect (i.e. an effect operating in both the educational policy and the journalistic fields which may be both cause and effect of the increasing integration between these two fields). Indeed, this whole second part of this chapter might be read in Bourdieurian terms as a tentative attempt to identify a cross-field effect across areas of social policy and public and private sectors which is leading to 'permanent amnesia' and absence of policy learning.

We suggest that, taken together, the prevalence of restructuring and new organisational practices, the institutional mobility of policy-makers and the emphasis on innovation within policy-making contexts offers a useful way of understanding and explaining loss of policy memory and absence of policy learning. A context of institutional instability and personnel mobility is unlikely to promote deliberative policy-making. A discourse in which a focus on innovation is dominant may also prompt fake amnesia; participants may remember salient past policy episodes but decide that it is in their best interests to 'forget', lest they be labelled defeatists for casting a questionable light on new, shiny policies.

Concluding comments

This chapter has (a) suggested that policy amnesia does operate within 14–19 policy-making and (b) proposed some explanations for this state of affairs. Assuming that a reasonably convincing case has been made for these propositions at least one further question arises. Does it matter that policy memory is lost?

Taking official rhetoric about evidence-informed policy at face value it must matter a great deal. Knowledge of what happened to cognate past policies is clearly a source of evidence for evaluating potential current policies. To state this is not to subscribe to the idea that 'learning from the past' is straightforward or unproblematic, but is to suggest that such learning has a contribution to make to policy-making. In the rational world of evidence-informed policy, policy-makers would be required to compare the contexts within which past and future policies were to be enacted in order to decide which particular facets of policy memory remain relevant. They would also be required to rigorously interrogate policy memories to ensure that they were accurate and comprehensive and could be clearly distinguished from policy myths. Such procedures, it could be argued, would make for better policy.

An alternative view would be that the notion of applying policy memory and the associated concept of policy learning to policy-making is based on naïve expectations. Policy-making on this view is highly volatile, contingent, context-bound and political. It involves practising the art of the possible in a policy-making context in which reflective policy learning from the past is currently a chimera – and likely to remain so.

A range of positions between these two formulations is possible, although the degree of policy learning which is possible is likely to vary according to the policy arena within which decisions are being taken, the characteristics of individual policies, the political and administrative timescales and time periods within which decisions are being taken and the nature and evidence for policy memories which can be drawn upon.

We end this chapter with brief reference to a paradox in the current policy-making process. Our focus in this chapter has been on forgetting, but an equally plausible chapter could be written about the importance of 'remembering' in policy-making on 14–19 education. Such a chapter would focus upon the significance of nostalgia in policy-making, for example: the golden age of A levels and grammar schools; the time when 5 per cent of an age cohort attended higher education; the time when teachers were free to design their own courses; the time when apprenticeships were a route into a job for life. This is not to suggest that 'remembering' is always a product of regressive sentimentality. Indeed if it were, the practice of policy learning would have little value. However, it is to suggest that 'remembering' and 'forgetting' are often not innocent practices but reflect the political, historical and educational contexts in which they take place.

This combination of forgetting *and* remembering is a fascinating policy phenomenon and is perhaps particularly pertinent to 14–19 education but its analysis will have to await another occasion.

References

Ball, S. (1981) *Beachside Comprehensive*. Cambridge: Cambridge University Press.

Bates, I. (1995) 'The competence movement: conceptualising recent research'. *Studies in Science Education*, 25, 39–68.

Bates, I., Clarke, J., Cohen, P., Finn, D., Moore, R. and Willis, P. (1984) *Schooling for the Dole*. London: Macmillan.

Benn, C. and Simon, B. (1970) *Half Way There: Report on the British comprehensive school*. London: McGraw-Hill.

Benn, T. (1989) *Office Without Power: Diaries 1968–72*. London: Arrow.

Brown, S. (1980) 'Key issues in the implementation of innovations in schools'. *Curriculum*, 1, 32–9.

Burgess, R. (1983) *Experiencing Comprehensive Education: A study of Bishop McGregor School*. London: Methuen.

Cohen, N. (2003) *Pretty Straight Guys*. London: Faber.

Crossman, R. (1979) *The Crossman Diaries: Selections from the diaries of a Cabinet Minister, 1964–1970*. London: Cape.

Dearing, R. (1993) *The National Curriculum and its Assessment*. York/London: NCC/SEAC.

Department of Education and Science (DES) (1979) *Aspects of Secondary Education in England: A survey by HM Inspectors of Schools*. London: HMSO.

— (1983) *Curriculum 11–16: Towards a statement of entitlement*. London: HMSO.

DES/DOE/Welsh Office (1991) *Education and Training for the 21st Century*. London: HMSO.

Department for Education and Skills (DfES) (2004) *14–19 Curriculum and Qualifications Reform: Final report of the Working Group on 14–19 Reform*. London: DfES.

— (2005a) *14–19 Education and Skills*. Cm 6476. London: HMSO.

— (2005b) *14–19 Education and Skills Implementation Plan*. London: DfES.

— (2005c) *Youth Matters*. London: DfES.

Dunford, J. (1998) *Her Majesty's Inspectorate of Schools since 1944: Standard bearers or turbulent priests?* London: Woburn Press.

Field, J. (1995) 'Reality testing in the workplace: are NVQs "employment-led"?'. In P. Hodkinson and M. Issitt (eds), *The Challenge of Competence*. London: Cassell.

Further Education Unit (FEU) (1979) *A Basis for Choice*. London: FEU.

Glennerster, H. (2001) 'Social policy'. In A. Seldon (ed.), *The Blair Effect*. London: Little, Brown.

Golden, S., O'Donnell, L. and Rudd, P. (2005) *Evaluation of the Increased Flexibility for 14–16 Year Olds Programme: The second year*. London: DfES.

Goodson, I. (2003) *Professional Knowledge, Professional Lives: Studies in education and change*. Maidenhead: Open University Press.

Higham, J. and Yeomans, D. (2005) *Collaborative Approaches to 14–19 Provision: An evaluation of the second year of the 14–19 Pathfinder Initiative*. London: DfES.

— (2006) *Emerging Provision and Practice in 14–19 Education and Training: A report on the third year of the 14–19 Pathfinder Initiative*. London: DfES.

Higham, J., Haynes, G., Wragg, C. and Yeomans, D. (2004) *14–19 Pathfinders: An evaluation of the first year. Research report RR504*. London: DfES.

Hodgson, A., Spours, K., Coffield, F., Steer, R., Finlay, I., Edward, S. and Gregson, M. (2005) *A New Learning and Skills Landscape? The LSC within the learning and skills sector*. Newcastle: Institute of Education/University of Strathclyde/University of Sunderland.

Kavanagh, D. and Seldon, A. (eds) (1989) *The Thatcher Effect*. Oxford: Oxford University Press.

Keep, E. (2005) 'Reflections on the curious absence of employers, labour market incentives and labour market regulation in English 14–19 policy: first signs of a change in direction?' *Journal of Education Policy*, 20, 533–53.

Lingard, B. and Rawolle, S. (2004) 'Mediatizing educational policy: the journalistic field, science policy, and cross-field effects'. *Journal of Education Policy*, 19, 361–80.

MSC/DES (Manpower Services Commission/Department of Education and Science) (1986) *Review of Vocational Qualifications in England and Wales*. London: HMSO.

Office for Standards in Education (Ofsted) (2005) *Developing a Coherent 14–19 Phase of Education and Training*. London: Ofsted.

Pollitt, C. (2000) 'Institutional amnesia: a paradox of the 'information age'? *Prometheus*, 18, 5–16.

Raggatt, P. and Williams, S. (1999) *Government, Markets and Vocational Qualifications: An anatomy of policy*. London: Falmer Press.

Rhodes, R. (2001) 'The Civil Service'. In Seldon, A. (ed.), *The Blair Effect*. London: Little, Brown.

Roberts, M. (2005) 'Employers' perspectives on current qualifications for the coloration industry'. Unpublished Ed. D. thesis, University of Leeds, Leeds.

Roe, P., Wiseman, J. and Costello, M. (2006) *Perceptions and Use of NVQs: A survey of employers in England*. London: DfES.

Sharp, P. (1998) 'The beginnings of GNVQs: an analysis of key determining events and factors'. *Journal of Education and Work*, 11, 293–311.

Shaw, K. and Robinson, F. (1998) 'Learning from experience? Reflections on two decades of British urban policy'. *Town Planning Review*, 69, 49–64.

Thatcher, M. (1995) *The Path to Power*. London: HarperCollins.

Tyack, D. and Cuban, L. (1995) *Tinkering toward Utopia*. Cambridge: Harvard University Press.

Wolf, A. (2002) *Does Education Matter? Myths about education and economic growth*. London: Penguin.

3 Learning from local experience: how effective is the Government's 14–19 learning model?

Ken Spours, Ann Hodgson and David Yeomans

The rise, fall and rise again of local innovation

The English education and training system, despite its drift towards centralism over the last two decades, has a long record of local innovation. Indeed, in the 30 years following World War II the dominant policy assumption was that innovation should be local and that particularly in relation to curriculum, pedagogy and assessment, there was no role for central government. Thus, George Tomlinson, Minister of Education in the post-war Labour Government proclaimed proudly that: 'Minister knows nowt about curriculum' (Richmond 1971: 71). The period is often described as an era of 'partnership' between central government, local government and teachers, but the relative powers of the partners was indicated by Bernard Donoughue, adviser to James Callaghan, likening the Department for Education and Science to a post box between the local authorities and the teachers' unions (Donoughue 1987). One consequence of this was that local innovation during that period took place in the virtual absence of a national policy framework. As we shall show, this is in stark contrast to the conditions in which local innovation is currently taking place. Into the 1980s, due to the role of the Technical and Vocational Education Initiative (TVEI) and the ability of awarding bodies to introduce new qualifications, practitioners continued to pioneer curriculum process-based reform – although TVEI also marked a significant stage in the transition from localism to centralism (Hodgson and Spours 1997; Yeomans 1998; Hodgson *et al.* 2004).

While local innovation was often celebrated during this period, it also came in for criticism for its variability, patchiness, absence of theoretical development and lack of systemic impact (e.g. Rudduck 1986; Hargreaves 1989). Thus, from a policy learning perspective, questions arise as to whether in the current context the strengths of local innovation can be accentuated and the weaknesses diminished.

The bottom-up movement receded in the early 1990s because of the impact of the accountability agenda with a focus on national examination results and performance tables and top-down qualifications reform (e.g. the introduction of GNVQs) and (at 14–16) the introduction of the National Curriculum in which professional practice became heavily determined by objectives-led curricula and mechanical, competence-based assessment. Nevertheless, even during this period, teachers in schools and colleges made problematical national initiatives more workable (Higham *et al.* 2002). By the end of the decade, it was the role of external examinations in GCSEs and under *Curriculum 2000* that drove professional practice (Hodgson and Spours 2003).

Local innovation is, however, back on the policy agenda because of 14–19 reform. The Government, in its 14–19 White Paper (DfES 2005a) and in the *14–19 Implementation Plan* (DfES 2005b), has clearly stated that it will not prescribe every step of the implementation of 14–19 reform. It recognises that localities will experience different challenges and will have to tailor their strategies accordingly. It is, therefore, up to local partnerships to decide how to deal with key local delivery issues such as governance arrangements (i.e. the co-ordination roles between local authorities, LSCs, institutions and wider stakeholders), the common curriculum framework, transport and so on. The *14–19 Implementation Plan* asserts that experience from Young Apprenticeships and the

Increased Flexibility Programme (IFP) indicates that 'locally agreed approaches have been most effective in enhancing curriculum breadth' (DfES 2005b: 19).

In stressing a role for local flexibility, the Government is keen to see the exchange of good practice between local 14–19 partnerships. It has, therefore, developed a 'learning model' comprising three closely related key elements:

- a number of 'best practice' partnerships derived mainly from 14–19 Pathfinders and Increased Flexibility projects;
- a programme of Learning Visits and other associated forms of support; and
- the encouragement of the widespread formation or growth of 14–19 partnerships in areas where they do not exist or are underdeveloped.

The three elements are intended to work closely together. The best practice partnerships provide system leadership, the Learning Visits and other forms of support act as mechanisms to disseminate best practice and the emerging 14–19 partnerships provide the contexts within which practice can be embedded and developed. The overall aim of the 'learning model' is to increase system capacity, especially in relation to vocational learning and the launch of the new specialised diplomas.

The emerging learning model rests on several inter-related assumptions. First, following a period of consultation starting in 2002 and finishing in 2004, the Government has set the framework of 14–19 policy and any freedoms of implementation and delivery will have to be within this framework. As noted above, this constitutes a marked contrast with the earlier era of local innovation. Second, practitioners will want to support the Government in its attempt to broaden 14–19 learning opportunities to motivate learners to help them progress and to make them more employment-ready. Third, practitioners and institutions will be willing and able to work in partnerships (and, in fact, will be required to do so) to achieve these aims. Fourth, certain 14–19 partnerships are deemed to be more advanced or to have more experience in the key areas of practice outlined in the 14–19 White Paper because of their involvement with the previous waves of 14–19 Pathfinders and the IFP. Fifth, the more advanced will want to teach those who are less advanced and the not so advanced will want to learn from those with expertise and experience. Once having attained knowledge about good practice, this can be creatively applied locally. Finally, learning and transfer can be achieved in less than two years in time for the introduction of the new specialised diplomas and other curriculum and qualification changes in 2008.

Using evidence available to date, this chapter undertakes a critical analysis of the three key elements of the Government's 'learning model' – best practice partnerships; Learning Visits and the emerging 14–19 partnerships – within the framework of assumptions outlined above, in order to assess the prognosis for practitioner and policy learning from local 14–19 experience. The chapter argues that there is little evidence that the Government is using these mechanisms to inform and shape national policy learning because of the 'set' nature of the policy agenda arising from the 14–19 White Paper and the rapid pace of reform indicated by the *14–19 Implementation Plan* for the period up until 2010. Moreover, in this policy context, the effectiveness of practitioner learning and good practice transfer is being compromised by limitations within the three elements of the Government's learning model. We go on to suggest that these constraints are resulting in learning that struggles to reach 'single-loop' characteristics and certainly does not accord with the 'double-loop' learning defined by Argyris and Schön (1978). As Chapter 1 explains, in the context of policy-making single-loop learning involves identifying problems in the implementation stage in order to correct them. Double-loop learning, on the other hand, involves understanding the problems of the policy in its wider context and may lead to re-examining the parameters of the policy itself. The chapter concludes by proposing five ways in which the 'learning model' might be improved in order to maximise learning from local experience in the period leading to the scheduled review of A levels in 2008.

14–19 best practice partnerships – policy learning or policy legitimation?

An integral building block of the 'learning model' is the concept of the 'pathfinder'. Used as a tool of 'experimentation' across a range of services (e.g. education and training, Children's Services, Home Office, Defra and so on), pathfinders are a policy-piloting strategy favoured by the Labour Government (Performance and Innovation Unit 2000). They are not, however, pilots in the strictest sense – i.e. testing predetermined interventions within tightly controlled conditions. Pathfinders are a more nebulous form of policy experimentation accorded several ambitious purposes: to develop 'best practice'; to provide a test-bed for policy initiatives; to reduce incidences of policy failure by providing swift feedback on the policy process prior to roll-out; to explore new solutions and to identify barriers to reform (Strategy Unit 2003).

Thus in relation to the development of 14–19, while the IFP also provided opportunities for local innovation the 14–19 Pathfinders were particularly significant in the development of the phase because of their broad role across the age range and the wide-ranging changes which they were potentially able to address. The 14–19 Pathfinders were intended to:

- test out a range of ideas and discover new ones
- develop best practice in 14–19 education and training to guide the steps to, and pace of, a national roll-out
- see how 14–19 policy will fit with other policies, identify barriers to a coherent 14–19 phase and design ways to overcome them

- show that a coherent 14–19 phase can be achieved nationally in a variety of locations with different social circumstances and different mixes of schools and colleges.

(Higham *et al.* 2004: 7)

In analysing the role of best practice partnerships in contributing to practitioner and policy learning, we make a distinction between the ability of these partnerships to carry out their function within the current policy climate and the extent to which government actually utilises the evidence they produce.

In relation to the ability of best practice partnerships to fulfil their role within the learning model, evaluative research suggests that this is compromised by the way in which they are funded. Evaluators point to evidence of local innovation in the hothouse conditions experienced by the Pathfinders where committed practitioners have been brought together with relatively lavish resources. Positive outcomes include the development of more practical and diverse approaches to learning and lessons on how to create and sustain different patterns of institutional collaboration (Higham and Yeomans 2006). Despite these messages, however, the difficulty then has to be faced of scaling up this type of innovation elsewhere, when the very conditions that produced the success are absent in replication.

Moreover, while 14–19 Pathfinders have been relatively generously resourced, their funding remained highly competitive and precarious. There was little incentive, therefore, for them to burden government with uncomfortable messages about barriers to innovation. In the competitive world of funding, it might be calculated that the best chance of securing future financing is to accentuate the positive and to place little emphasis on the inhibiting factors. Put another way – the best practice partnership function of trying to demonstrate the possible could actually undermine the desire for policy learning.

In addition, the precarious funding of 14–19 Pathfinders and the rapid nature of 14–19 policy-making means that these exemplars of innovation can come and go. They are often not in the position, therefore, to form sustainable networks of trust. Pathfinder evaluators sum up the transient nature of this aspect of 'policy piloting' in an era of policy busyness and initiative overload:

> As the 14–19 Pathfinders initiative recedes into history and other developments in 14–19 come to the fore it will inevitably become more difficult to identify specific aspects which have been replicated since these will have become inextricably entangled with newer developments located in different contexts. Therefore to look for systemic effects from the programme may be neither feasible nor desirable.
>
> (Higham and Yeomans 2006: 56)

Despite the high profile and investment in best practice partnerships the Government appears to have made limited use of them in terms of policy learning. These partnerships have been given some systemic functions insofar as they are intended to identify barriers and show linkages between policies. This is part of their role in reducing the possibility of gross policy failure and offering some sort of 'insurance policy' by providing feedback for policy-makers early in the implementation process (Strategy Unit 2003). But what do the best practice partnerships actually tell policy-makers and how are they used? The 14–19 White Paper made 12 references to the 14–19 Pathfinders and IFP. It reported that a great deal of innovation was taking place and concluded from this that the proposed policy framework could work (e.g. 'autonomous' institutions can collaborate). There were no other indications of what the Government had learned from the best practice partnerships and there was certainly no discussion about barriers. This, it might be argued, could be because the main barriers frustrating change and improvement derive from the Government's own policies (e.g. the refusal to reform general qualifications; the encouragement of institutional competition; the absence of a coherent and stable 14–19 funding mechanism).

The learning role of the best practice partnerships is intimately tied up with Government approaches towards consultation processes; both are meant to inform policy. The 14–19 consultation process since the first 2002 Green Paper has, however, been fragmented rather than iterative. The 14–19 White Paper was published following evaluation reports of the first waves of Pathfinders and Increased Flexibility projects (Higham *et al.* 2004; Golden *et al.* 2004, 2005a) but before the publication of three further reports (Higham and Yeomans 2005, 2006; Golden *et al.* 2005b). In fact, there was no clear line of evaluation or consultation between the Green Paper *14–19 Education: Extending opportunities, raising standards* (DfES 2002) and the publication of the 14–19 White Paper in 2005. In its Green Paper response document *14–19: Opportunity and Excellence* (DfES 2003a) the Government admitted that the 2002 Green Paper lacked a coherent long-term vision. Spurred on by the A level grading crisis of 2003, Ministers proposed the formation of the Tomlinson Working Group to map a future strategy. After toiling for 18 months, the central recommendation of the Working Group on 14–19 Reform, for a unified and inclusive diploma system (Working Group on 14–19 Reform 2004), was rejected by a new set of education Ministers in the run up to a general election. As Chapter 1 explains, the main force behind 14–19 strategy was not reflections on past policies or practice but the pressure of politics. By the time of the *14–19 Implementation Plan*, the idea of 'learning' from best practice partnerships was confined entirely to practitioner learning and good practice transfer with no reference to national policy-makers or national policy learning. Nor was there any indication of how far pathfinders could develop different types of practice.

As their name implies, best practice partnerships are also intended to develop and disseminate best practice as part of practitioner learning. The issue of practice transfer will be discussed in the next section on Learning Visits. There is, however, the problem of the concept of 'best practice' itself. Originating in the

private sector as a tool to benchmark performance against competitors, the concept of 'best practice' has entered popular parlance in the public sector as part of the Government's agenda of driving up performance (Brannan *et al.* 2006). Seen as a subtler tool than targets and the accountability agenda, best practice describes a process in which innovation is stimulated, identified and then disseminated by central government, leading to widespread improvement (Newman *et al.* 2000). The concept also has the advantage of coinciding with the commonsense notion that it is both sensible and possible to learn in a relatively unproblematic way from those who are 'getting it right'.

Newman and colleagues note, however, that best practice and innovation have been treated as synonymous, whereas they should be regarded as distinct. Innovation is new practice whereas 'best practice is the adoption of a new practice/policy through following some generally accepted view among practitioners of what is a state of the art approach' (Brannan *et al.* 2006: 3). Furthermore, the research by Brannan *et al.* confirms the findings of Fielding and colleagues (2005) who found that concepts of 'best practice' are more effectively communicated laterally through 'networks of trust' and that dissemination from central government through best practice manuals has proved somewhat less useful. The Government, however, still relies heavily on good/best practice manuals as a means of dissemination. Commenting on this, the authors of the most recent Pathfinder evaluation (Higham and Yeomans 2006) point to the DfES 14–19 Gateway website with its section on good practice which details the Learning Visits, a good practice manual together with case studies and video clips, based on the practice in 14–19 Pathfinders. The evaluators go on to remark, however, that they have no evidence of how many people have used these resources and in what way.

In concluding this analysis of best practice partnerships and their contribution to the learning model, we highlight the limitations of this 'rational' model. Best practice partnerships are part of the

rational model of a 'what works' approach to policy-making – the idea of trialling and piloting and then disseminating in order to bring about implementation on a larger scale.

As we have seen, however, the 'rational' aspect of the model is weakened by three major problems. First, policy learning is affected by the politicisation of policy-making – set policy agendas which have rejected the professional voice; politically determined timetables and an unwillingness, at least at this point, to question the effects of key policy levers and drivers that mould institutional behaviour. The 'rational' model of policy-making is meant to be procedural (i.e. waiting for evidence from piloting before rolling out national programmes). However, the Government's preoccupation with political considerations encourages it continually to break these rules.

The second problem is that the best practice partnerships have been unable to pilot policies in optimum conditions because they are being asked to experiment with half-finished reforms (e.g. they have to simulate the implementation of specialised diplomas when their design has not yet been agreed) and they do not have significant control over the policy factors that drive institutional behaviour or the take-up of qualifications.

The third problem arises from assumptions about practitioner and institutional learning. Best practice partnerships are part of what can be termed 'elite teaching' – more innovative institutions teach less innovative ones. This has become an increasingly ubiquitous feature of government policy as represented by the establishment, for example, of specialist schools, beacon schools, Centres of Vocational Excellence (COVEs) and leading edge partnerships. Despite the ubiquity of this elite practitioner and institutional 'teaching' model there is little evidence that a great deal of progress has been made in conceptualising and then implementing the ways in which best practice can be transferred and learning can take place. Recent research (e.g. Fielding *et al.* 2005; Higham and Yeomans 2006) suggests that this is not the most effective way of

organising practitioner learning because of the lack of ownership, the risk of mechanical borrowing and the inability to reproduce the conditions under which 'best practice' emerged on a wider scale. We expand on this issue in the next section.

While the best practice partnership concept has its merits as a source of local innovation we argue that it suffers from the effects of the wider politicised policy landscape. Moreover, the partnership experience accords with findings from policy and practice transfer in local regeneration programmes where it was also recognised that pathfinder-type initiatives tend to function more as a source of policy legitimation than as a means of policy learning or analysis (Joseph Rowntree Foundation 2000). Their experience too begs the question of whether best practice partnerships can, indeed, pave the way for others or whether everyone has to find their own way by reflecting upon their unique as well as their shared conditions.

Learning Visits

As a related element of the best practice partnership concept, the DfES programme of Learning Visits, represents 'a mechanism for enabling everyone to learn from the areas that have made the most progress' (DfES 2005b: 9). Ten best practice partnerships (seven involved in 14–19 Pathfinders and three in IFP) presently offer Learning Visits to 14–19 partnerships across the country. Visits last a day, though, in theory at least, there are opportunities for longer-term relationships between schools and colleges.

In addition, it is proposed to establish four types of networks to support 14–19 White Paper developments:

- networks to support learning transfer from the Learning Visits
- networks linking schools, colleges and the Diploma Development Partnerships that are currently designing the 14 lines of the proposed specialised diplomas

- sector-wide networks of COVEs and the newly established Skills Academies to promote quality vocational provision within the diplomas
- regional networks of subject coaches to ensure the adoption of good practice.

The Government has also funded the Learning and Skills Network (LSN) to run a '14–19 programme of support for delivery of change on the ground'. This is designed to provide schools and colleges with the help they need to deliver the type of broad and flexible curriculum that features in the *14–19 Education and Skills* White Paper and the resulting *14–19 Implementation Plan* (LSN 2006). This help is provided through consultancies, materials and workshops. According to the 'timeline for reform' (DfES 2005b: 23), it is intended that the Learning Visits, networks and LSN support programme will facilitate preparation and disseminate good practice in time for the first wave of specialised diplomas in 2008.

The Government is undoubtedly committed to enabling practitioner learning from local practice within the framework of established policy. Moreover, the programme of Learning Visits is underway and is proving popular with groups of practitioners. The question is not whether learning is taking place, but whether the learning model will prove effective in establishing improvements in 14–19 learning, provision and policy. In terms of evidence, it is simply too early to make a judgement. However, the assumptions of the Government's model can be tested against recent research on the transfer of good practice (Fielding *et al.* 2005) and on the experience of 14–19 Pathfinders (Higham and Yeomans 2006).

On the basis of wide-ranging research evidence (i.e. interviews with 120 practitioners who have tried good practice transfer; data from over 30 beacon institutions, recipients of best practice scholarships and the outcomes of seminars to discuss interim findings), Fielding and colleagues from the University of Sussex and Demos arrived at the conclusions summarised in the first column of

Table 3.1 (Fielding *et al.* 2005). These are compared with features and conditions within the Government's 14–19 good practice learning model listed in the second column.

Table 3.1 Transferring and learning from good practice

Factors influencing the transfer of good practice*	Government's 14–19 good practice learning model
Joint practice development rather than practice transfer	Practice transfer focused
Development and continuity of trust relationships built on previous experience	New and possibly temporary learning relationships based around the Learning Visits
Learners are engaged due to involvement in joint planning of the learning	Learners are the recipients of 'good practice'
Understanding time and addressing the issue of lack of time	Politically inspired deadlines (e.g. 2008 for the introduction of the first five specialised diplomas and all to be introduced by 2010) which leave little time for consultation or policy learning
Positive teacher and institutional identity through a 'non-badging' approach	Potential for labelling institutions as 'advanced' and 'less advanced'
Supportive structures for transfer – time, communication, funding and technology	Limitations in all of these
Challenges of evaluation and seeing whether good practice transfer actually takes place	Too early to tell but tradition of evaluation established through 14–19 Pathfinders and IFP

*Source: Fielding *et al.* (2005).

The main difference between the joint practice development advocated by the research findings and government-sponsored practice transfer is one of mutual engagement and time. Learning Visits are based on hierarchical, temporary and time-constrained learning relationships rather than on mutually supportive relationships fostered over time.

These differences can also be conceptualised in terms of the distinctions between 'acquisitive' and 'participatory' learning made by Sfard (1998) and modified by Hager (2005) through the addition of 'constructivist' learning. While these positions conflate important distinctions and complexities concerning learning (McGuinness 2005) they can be used to examine dominant assumptions within learning programmes. Table 3.1 shows how Fielding *et al.* emphasised the participatory character of learning through their emphasis on joint practice development and the joint planning of learning. In contrast, the emerging 14–19 learning model privileges the acquisitive model through the Learning Visits as well as other aspects of the support provided, such as the manual of good practice and other on-line or printed materials. Recipients are envisaged as essentially soaking up information about 14–19 best practice, which it is assumed can then be applied relatively unproblematically in their own contexts.

This characterisation of the dominant model of learning embodied in the 14–19 learning model was confirmed in the case of one particular Learning Visit to a best practice partnership, which comprised a PowerPoint slideshow of no less than 67 slides delivered over a five-hour period. The recipients would certainly have gone away somewhat awestruck by the accomplishments of the innovating institutions. However, how much they would have taken away to transfer to their own context is less clear. The question of 'practice transfer' was simply not on the agenda, it was assumed.

This is not to say that some participatory and constructivist learning may not have taken place both during and after Learning Visits. Nor is it to suggest that acquisitive learning is inherently

inferior to other types of learning. However, we do suggest that a learning programme based predominantly on a view of learning as acquisition is not appropriate for supporting the establishment of partnerships where deep, grounded contextual understandings of local circumstances are essential and, therefore, where participatory and constructivist learning needs to be prevalent.

Moreover, research evidence on partnership building emphasises the importance of time in developing trust, shared understandings and appropriate structures (Hudson and Hardy 2002). Participatory and constructivist support for these processes is likely to be labour-intensive, since it needs to be carefully tailored to particular local contexts. There are elements of such customised support with the 14–19 learning model but the overall emphasis is upon a set menu. The effectiveness of Learning Visits will depend not only on the quality of the visit experience itself, which will in turn be influenced by implicit models of learning, but also on factors related to those who want to learn. Learning Visits, by their very nature, are fleeting and compressed learning experiences.

The DfES has stated that it would like to see a follow-up process to the Learning Visits but it is difficult to see how a limited number of busy best practice partnerships will have the time to consolidate multiple learning relationships within the time constraints under which they are forced to operate.

The effectiveness of practice transfer, as the research illustrates, depends on a wider range of factors. In addition to those listed in the Fielding *et al.* research, our consultancy work with 14–19 partnerships suggests that factors affecting practitioner learning include the degree of cohesion of the partnership seeking advice and how far it has clarified its aims and questions. Many partnerships are at an early stage of development and may, from our observations, be simply casting around to learn 'randomly' rather than seeking concrete solutions to help them progress in a particular area or solve an identified problem. This tendency may be exacerbated when partnerships have come into being to meet the demands of national policy or to gain access to particular funding streams rather than growing out of shared understandings of local needs and aspirations.

In addition and crucially, 14–19 partnerships are seeking solutions to problems that cannot be solved by examining the practice of others, because the issues that exercise everyone most (e.g. the nature of qualifications and assessment, institutional competition, performance measures and funding instability) emanate from policy itself and the role of key policy levers and drivers beyond the immediate control of even the most innovative 14–19 partnerships.

Reflection so far on the limitations of the Government's learning model, involving 14–19 best practice partnerships and Learning Visits, points to the important role of all 14–19 partnerships, their cohesion, their capacity to learn from their own experiences as well as the experiences of others and their ability to exercise some local control over external national policy levers and drivers that mould institutional behaviour.

14–19 partnerships – learning within weakly collaborative arrangements

The third element of the Government's learning model is the idea of institutional collaboration and partnership to stimulate and replicate good practice. Partnership has become a key element of government social policy (e.g. Balloch and Taylor 2001; Glendinning *et al.* 2002) and has become increasingly ubiquitous within education and training policy, for example in relationship to networked learning projects (e.g. Kerr *et al.* 2003), professional learning communities (e.g. Bolam *et al.* 2005) and Education Improvement Partnerships (DfES 2005c). The importance of partnership working has been further emphasised with the adoption of the *Every Child Matters* agenda (DfES 2003b) with its focus on multi-agency working.

Collaboration between 14–19 institutions has become a policy priority because the Government realises that the offer of a local entitlement, including all 14 lines of specialised diplomas cannot be effectively delivered by a single institution. Schools, colleges and work-based learning providers are being 'expected' to form and to further develop local 14–19 partnerships on an area basis (DfES 2005b). Furthermore, it will not be possible for institutions to pass through the Specialised Diploma Gateway and thus offer the diplomas unless they can demonstrate that they 'are working together, with firm collaboration arrangements in place' (DfES 2006: 16). While this insistence upon the establishment of partnerships demonstrates the importance which the Government attaches to it, there is something distinctly odd about *ordering* institutions to form partnerships. Of course, in many localities institutions may not need to be ordered to collaborate, while elsewhere the Government may be pushing at an open door. However, the approach does also risk the possibility of promoting contrived collegiality (see Hargreaves 1994) in which collaboration is simulated in order to obtain funding or pass through the Specialised Diploma Gateway.

At the same time, however, the Government still believes in market mechanisms for driving up the standard of provision and so promotes contestability of provision and institutional competition through the introduction of new sixth forms, academies and skills centres (DfES 2004).

Therefore 14–19 collaborative arrangements are being developed in a policy climate that has an acute balance of enabling and inhibiting features. On the positive side, Pathfinder evaluations (e.g. Higham and Yeomans 2005) suggest that factors assisting collaboration and, thereby, producing a potential climate for learning are: a history of collaboration in the locality; shared aims and objectives; strong local leadership; access to additional funding; and an absence of hierarchy between participating institutions. Many of these factors concern the internal dynamics of partnership arrangements, though these can vary considerably between partnerships and are susceptible to change and disruption.

Balanced against these are powerful external inhibiting factors: unreformed general qualifications; institutional competition; and performance measures that weaken collaboration (Hodgson and Spours 2006). Government policy, which has left GCSEs and A levels relatively unchanged and which encourages the establishment of new sixth forms, risks being interpreted by selective and academically high performing schools as a message that they can have a minimal involvement in what looks like a 14–19 vocational reform agenda. On the other hand, those institutions that do identify with the vocational emphasis of the *14–19 Implementation Plan*, but are pressured by performance tables and the need to improve their GCSE 5 A*–C grades, can make decisions which also frustrate genuine collaboration. For example, schools may decide unilaterally to offer a range of 'weakly vocational' subjects such as business, IT and leisure and tourism qualifications (these subjects can be offered as different-sized GNVQs, equivalent to either two or four GCSEs) to boost their GCSE points scores while, at the same time, deciding to decant their most disaffected learners into link schemes with colleges. Moreover, in a climate in which institutional commitment to collaboration can be equivocal, organisational complexities, such as common timetabling, may exercise an additional deterrent effect.

Government, however, appears to have little understanding of the relationship between external policy levers and drivers, or this kind of institutional decision-making and how it affects practitioner and policy learning, despite its continued reliance on these mechanisms as the preferred mode of governance within the Learning and Skills Sector (Steer *et al.* 2006). Research on 14–19 collaboration over the last two years (Hayward *et al.* 2005) suggests that the capacity for 14–19 partnerships to learn from their experience depends not only on their ability to reflect on issues of practice but also on their capacity to understand and to be able to act upon aspects of national policy that currently constrain innovation.

At this stage in the policy process, enabling factors for

institutional collaboration appear to be largely related to the internal dynamics of a partnership and the inhibiting factors appear to be mainly external. Our assessment is that external factors are more powerful than internal ones and it is this adverse balance that renders 14–19 partnerships 'weakly collaborative' (Hayward *et al.* 2005). An important question will be the power exercised by the statutory nature of the 14–19 Entitlement and the role of the Specialised Diploma Gateway that will only allow institutions to offer the first wave of specialised diplomas if there is evidence of area-wide collaboration. These two measures may, indeed, have a regulatory effect on those wanting to be involved, but may have little power to affect decision-making in those institutions that do not identify with 14–19 vocational provision. The entitlement, which focuses heavily on the vocational specialised diplomas, could end up codifying an institutional academic/vocational divide.

Elsewhere, we have argued that this Government has made 'half-right' policy assumptions about learners and their learning (Hodgson *et al.* 2006). The same assessment could equally be applied to their assumptions about practitioner and policy learning from local experience. The Government is probably largely correct in assuming that practitioners want to learn from one another, but the most effective learning appears to take place through sustained, open and strong learning relationships rather than through time-constrained Learning Visits and best practice manuals. The Government is also correct in assuming that trialling, experimentation and piloting can assist in policy development, but it seems unable to facilitate these activities in any meaningful way in the 14–19 phase due to its rushed and politically informed reform agenda.

Improving practitioner and policy learning in the wider policy process

Despite the aims of the three-dimensional 14–19 learning model to improve both practice and policy, Ministers seem far more committed to fostering practitioner learning, in what they see as the implementation phase of 14–19 reform, than to national policy learning from local experience. Moreover, while the DfES may be putting in place structures for practitioner learning, the rapidity of the policy process prevents this from happening effectively. Seen through the lens of single- and double-loop learning (Argyris and Schön 1978) the Government sees a role for single-loop learning to provide 'corrections' in the 14–19 implementation phase. On the other hand, it appears to have little or no commitment to double-loop learning that would pose challenges to the parameters of policy. The experience of its learning model to date suggests that single-loop learning will be an achievement. With consultations on specialised diplomas lasting days rather than months (e.g. the consultation on Level 1 Specialised Diploma models had a 48-hour reply window); with the new wave of best practice partnerships being asked to trial unfinished qualification designs; and 14–19 partnerships being asked to sign up to the Specialised Diploma Gateway before they know what the new qualifications involve, we may even be looking at 'half-loop' learning.

The limitations of the prevailing model provide clues as to what is required to promote more effective practice and policy learning from local experience and innovation. Five key areas of required action emerge from the analysis in this chapter:

1. It will be important to slow down the reform process so that the fundamental building blocks of 14–19 reform can be modelled, created, discussed and piloted in order to 'grind out' design mistakes. This more deliberative process did not take place under *Curriculum 2000* and there is every chance that the same mistakes could be repeated with the specialised diplomas. Moreover, a longer and more deliberative approach is particularly warranted in the case of the specialised diplomas because of the untested way in which these qualifications have been designed. The need for a longer learning process is more pressing because of the

relative inexperience of the diploma designers. Diploma Development Partnerships, led by the newly formed Sector Skills Councils, have been put firmly in the driving seat while a back-seat role has been allocated to more experienced and expert organisations such as QCA and the awarding bodies.

2. Longer implementation timescales are also needed to provide a framework for the creation of sustainable mutual learning networks and partnerships to exchange innovative practice in the way that research suggests is likely to be effective. More time for reform would also provide the space for effective single-loop learning.

3. Double-loop learning will be the key to more effective practitioner learning from local practice. Some control needs to be exercised by 14–19 partnerships over the policy parameters that affect innovation. Key to this, for example, will be their ability to set up area-wide accountability measures to encourage more collective institutional behaviour and to broaden the scope of collaboration. The *14–19 Implementation Plan* states that there will be adjustments to accountability mechanisms in 2007, but it is not clear whether the Government is prepared to go as far as promoting policy levers and drivers that will significantly strengthen institutional collaboration over competition.

4. The Government needs to show a greater commitment to national policy learning from local innovation rather than being content with best practice transfer. This means creating more effective forums for policy feedback. Presently, this appears to be a somewhat random activity confined to selected groups of practitioners and policy-makers, some of whom are constrained by dependence on funding. There is no systematic wider process of feedback because ministers and senior civil servants are reluctant to re-engage in debates about the Tomlinson reform proposals, yet these curriculum and qualification issues are crucial

because of the level of support for a more unified approach to 14–19 reform. The absence of this kind of dialogue is leading to a significant 'narrative gap' between the most active and innovative members of the profession and national policy-makers.

5. The Government will need to show, at a minimum, tolerance of the variations of pace and direction of development that will be the inevitable consequences of enabling greater local innovation. This tolerance will need to be reflected in the operation of national policy levers and regulations. More positively, the Government may wish actively to celebrate such variations and defend divergences of practice across different 14–19 partnerships. There are clearly issues around the degrees and forms of variation that might be considered acceptable. As we noted early in this chapter, some critics asserted that the variations were too wide in the earlier era of localism. One of the functions of the double-loop policy learning advocated above is that it would provide a basis upon which debates (involving national and local policy-makers and practitioners) could be conducted about the degrees of local variation acceptable to national policy.

Stepping back, it seems clear that learning from local experience involves not only providing the conditions for practitioner learning but also a deep-seated commitment to deliberative and collaborative policy learning in the broader sense. The local and national are inextricably linked in the policy process. Practitioners have historically provided a rich source of innovation within the English education and training system and the implementation phase of 14–19 reform has invited them, once again, to play a part. To date, however, the Government's learning model is encouraging only 'restricted' and 'half-loop' learning, whereas, with more professional trust and less politics, it could be facilitating a far more effective learning process.

References

Argyris, C. and Schön, D. (1978) *Organizational Learning: A theory of action perspective*. Reading, Mass: Addison Wesley.

Balloch, S. and Taylor, M. (eds) (2001) *Partnership Working: Policy and practice*. Bristol: Policy Press.

Bolam, R., McMahon, A., Stoll, L., Wallace, M., Hawkey, K. and Greenwood, A. (2005) *Creating and Sustaining Effective Professional Learning Communities*. DfES Research Report RR637, University of Bristol. Online. Available HTTP: www.dfes.gov.uk/research/data/uploades/RB637.pdf (accessed 13 September 2006).

Brannan, T., Durose, C., John, P. and Wolman, H. (2006) 'Assessing best practice as a means of innovation'. Paper prepared for presentation at the Annual Conference of the Urban Affairs Association, Montreal, Canada, April 22.

Department for Education and Skills (DfES) (2002) *14–19 Education: Extending opportunities, raising standards*. London: DfES.

— (2003a) *14–19: Opportunity and Excellence; government response to the 14–19 Green Paper*. London: DfES.

— (2003b) *Every Child Matters*. London: DfES.

— (2004) *Five Year Strategy for Children and Learners*. London: DfES.

— (2005a) *14–19 Education and Skills*. London: DfES.

— (2005b) *The 14–19 Implementation Plan*. London: DfES.

— (2005c) *Education Improvement Partnerships: Local collaboration for school improvement and better service delivery*. London: DfES.

— (2006) *The Specialised Diploma Gateway*. London: DfES.

Donoughue, B. (1987) *Prime Minister: The conduct of policy under Harold Wilson and James Callaghan*. London: Jonathan Cape.

Fielding, M., Bragg, S., Craig, J., Cunningham, I., Eraut, M., Gillinson, D., Horne, M., Robinson, C. and Thorp, J. (2005) *Factors Influencing the Transfer of Good Practice*. RR615, University of Sussex and Demos. London: DfES.

Glendinning, C., Powell, M. and Rummery, K. (eds) (2002) *Partnerships, New Labour and the governance of welfare*. Bristol: Policy Press.

Golden, S., Nelson, J., O'Donnell, L. and Morris, M. (2004) *Evaluation of Increased Flexibility for 14–16 Year Olds Programme: The first year*. RR511. Nottingham: DfES.

Golden, S., O'Donnell, L. and Rudd, P. (2005a) *Evaluation of the Increased Flexibility for 14–16 Year Olds Programme: The second year*. London: DfES.

83

Golden, S., O'Donnell, L., Benton, T. and Rudd, P. (2005b) *Evaluation of Increased Flexibility for 14 to 16 Year Olds Programme: Outcomes for the first cohort.* London: DfES.

Hager, P. (2005). 'Current theories of workplace learning: a critical assessment'. In N. Bascia, A. Cumming, A. Datnow, K. Leithwood and D. Livingstone (eds), *International Handbook of Educational Policy.* Berlin: Springer.

Hargreaves, A. (1989) *Curriculum and Assessment Reform.* Milton Keynes: Open University Press.

— (1994) *Changing Teachers, Changing Times : Teachers' work and culture in the post-modern age.* London: Cassell.

Hayward, G., Hodgson, A., Johnson, J., Oancea, A., Pring, R., Spours, K., Wright, S. and Wilde, S. (2005) *Annual Report of the Nuffield 14–19 Review 2004–5.* OUDES: University of Oxford.

Higham, J. and Yeomans, D. (2005) *Collaborative Approaches to 14–19 Provision: An evaluation of the second year of the 14–19 Pathfinder Initiative.* Research Report RR642. London: DfES.

— (2006) *Emerging Provision and Practice in 14–19 Education and Training: A report on the evaluation of the third year of the 14–19 Pathfinder Initiative.* London: DfES.

Higham, J., Sharp, P. and Yeomans, D. (2002) *Changing the 14–19 School Curriculum in England: Lessons from successive reforms.* Research Report to the Economic and Social Research Council (ESRC). Swindon: ESRC.

Higham, J., Haynes, G., Wragg, C. and Yeomans, D. (2004) *14–19 Pathfinders: An evaluation of the first year.* Research Report RR504. London: DfES.

Hodgson, A. and Spours, K. (eds) (1997) *Dearing and Beyond: 14–19 qualifications, frameworks and systems.* London: Kogan Page.

— (2003) *Beyond A Levels: Curriculum 2000 and the reform of 14–19 qualifications.* London: Kogan Page.

— (2006) 'The organization of 14–19 education and training in England: beyond weakly collaborative arrangements'. *Journal of Education and Work*, 19 (4), 325–42.

Hodgson, A., Howieson, C., Raffe, D., Spours, K. and Tinklin, T. (2004) 'Post-16 curriculum and qualifications reforms in England and Scotland: lessons from home international comparisons'. *Journal of Education and Work*, 17 (4), 441–65.

Hodgson, A., Steer, R., Spours, K., Edward, S., Coffield, F., Finlay, I. and Gregson, M. (forthcoming) 'Learners in the English learning and skills sector: the implications of half-right policy assumptions'. *Oxford Review of Education.*

Hudson, B. and Hardy, B. (2002) 'What is a "successful" partnership and how can it be measured?' In C. Glendinning, M. Powell and K. Rummery (eds), *Partnerships, New Labour and the Governance of Welfare*. Bristol: Policy Press.

Joseph Rowntree Foundation (2000) *Policy Transfer between Local Regeneration Partnerships*. York: Joseph Rowntree Foundation.

Kerr, D., Aiston, S., White, K., Holland, M. and Grayson, H. (2003) *Review of Networked Learning Communities: Literature review*. Slough: NFER.

Learning and Skills Network (LSN) (2006) *14–19 Programme of Support for Delivery of Change on the Ground*. Online. Available HTTP: http://www.vocationallearning.org.uk/14–19/ (accessed 5 July 2006).

McGuinness, C. (2005) 'Behind the acquisition metaphor: conceptions of learning and learning outcomes in TLRP school-based projects'. *The Curriculum Journal*, 16, 31–47.

Newman, J., Raine, J. and Skelcher, C. (2000) *Innovation and Best Practice in Local Government: A research report*. London: Department for Transport, Local Government and the Regions (DETR).

Performance and Innovation Unit (2000) *Adding It Up: Improving analysis and modelling in central government*. London: Cabinet Office.

Richmond, K. (1971). *The School Curriculum*. London: Methuen.

Rudduck, J. (1986) *Understanding Curriculum Change*. Sheffield: University of Sheffield.

Sfard, A. (1998) On two metaphors for learning and the dangers of choosing just one. *Educational Researcher*, 27, 4–13.

Steer, R., Spours, K., Hodgson, A., Finlay, I., Coffield, F., Edward, S. and Gregson, M. (2006) 'Modernisation and the role of policy levers in the Learning and Skills Sector'. BERA Paper, Institute of Education, University of Strathclyde and University of Sunderland.

Strategy Unit (2003) *Trying It Out – The role of 'pilot' in policy-making. Report of a Review of Government Pilots*. London: Cabinet Office.

Working Group on 14–19 Reform (2004) *14–19 Curriculum and Qualifications Reform: Final report*. London: DfES.

Yeomans, D. (1998) 'Constructing vocational education: from TVEI to GNVQ'. *Journal of Education and Work*, 11, 127–49.

4 Turbulence masquerading as change: exploring 14–19 policy

Jacky Lumby and Nick Foskett

Introduction

Since Margaret Thatcher's first term as Prime Minister in 1979, many policy innovations to develop and reform 14–19 education can be identified in the strategies of successive governments, irrespective of political persuasion. These have ranged from the use of agencies and initiatives as a vehicle for change (e.g. through the Manpower Services Commission), to major adjustments in education structure/organisation (e.g. through the freeing of post-16 colleges from local education authority (LEA) control), to attempts at significant curriculum change (e.g. the introduction of GNVQs and, later, *Curriculum 2000*).

However, despite this prima facie appearance of continuous and radical change, a more careful analysis of policy evolution suggests that this period has in fact been one of turbulence masquerading as change. This chapter suggests that the conviction that change has been persistent and significant is not fundamentally valid, and challenges generally accepted perceptions of policy change and its effects. It explores how the busyness of policy change conceals the steady state of underlying values and calculations of advantage to those groups with most power. Contrary to the common assumption that there is an absence of learning from policy change and its effects, we argue that policy learning does take place but as learning of a particular character. Rather than deploring an absence of learning those seeking to influence policy must instead pay greater attention to the nature of the learning. Here we explore what concepts of learning and particularly adult learning may be most relevant or whether the notion of policy learning demands a different conceptualisation.

The waves of policy development

Across the whole of the education arena in England, the period since James Callaghan's Ruskin Speech in 1976 has been portrayed as one of rapid, continuous and fundamental change. Ruskin marked the end of the post-war settlement (Salter and Tapper 1981) that had left public sector services in the hands of the professionals to design, deliver and develop the service according to their own judgements of need. It also marked the formal establishment of a utilitarian view of key public services as education, in particular, was identified as failing to deliver the skills and knowledge essential both for an economy seeking a strong position in a globalised political world and to meet the social agenda of government. The period of debate this ushered in was followed by the election of the Thatcher Government in 1979, bringing with it an era of interventionist policies, centralisation of authority and the marginalisation of professional educators as power was wrested from the perceived snares of producer capture. Education and training for 14–19 year olds has been a significant battlefield in this ideological war, and analysis of the changing policy scene for 14–19 provides a microcosm of policy development in the wider educational arena in the UK.

A common view of those working in the 14–19 sector is that they have been the victims of innovation overload as a result of policy development throughout the last two decades (Goulding *et al.* 1998). This presents a vision of continuous change, of the demand for new systems of organisation or practice before previous waves of change have had a chance to become embedded. Policy innovation and reform is depicted as endemic both within DfES and its predecessors and also in the wide range of quangos through which policy is enacted and refined. Changes in practice or organisation require periods of enhanced activity to implement them, and there is a perception that the 14–19 sector has been required to work at a much higher level of intensity continuously as a result of policy development. Policy turbulence is seen, therefore, to have produced a higher energy operational environment for the sector.

Closer analysis of this policy turbulence suggests that it has a distinctive structure and pattern. In taking a macro-scale view of this turbulence we might characterise the evolution of the 14–19 sector in terms of three waves of change, each focused on a specific dimension of the education and training system, each seeking to address some of the perceived failings of the other waves. It would be naïve, of course, to believe that any government has a long-term vision that planned these waves over a quarter of a century. Nevertheless, there has been a strong pattern of development that has been sequential and has transcended changes in government. The waves have not been sequential in a strict 'end on' sense in that they have overlapped and been interwoven. All persist to some extent through to the present. However, the initiation of each can be identified as the principal drive of specific periods of time, and their ascendancy, zenith and decline can be traced through the landscape of 14–19.

Wave 1 – initiatives and agencies for change

At the beginning of the Thatcher era, the chosen strategy was to charge the responsibility for change to government agencies and to promote new initiatives to deliver the desired outcomes. Three distinctive elements of this strategy can be identified. First, government sought to spread authority for education away from the Department of Education and Science (DES) to include those departments responsible for economic development, the Department of Employment and the Department for Trade and Industry (DTI). Education was seen to be a key economic driver and hence too important to be left solely to educationalists to manage. Secondly, government delegated considerable policy power to quangos, principally the Manpower Services Commission. Their role was to manage developments in key areas through mechanisms of direct policy intervention, while ensuring arm's-length accountability for government. Thirdly, government chose direct intervention through the establishment of funded programmes, with the development of vocational training schemes such as the Youth Opportunities Programmes (YOP), its successor the Youth Training Scheme (YTS), and TVEI (the Technical and Vocational Education Initiative).

Wave 2 – structural change

By the late 1980s increasing recognition of the persistence of some of the underlying issues with 14–19 education and training, combined with strong negative views of the effectiveness of both the schemes and the agencies that had appeared in the first wave of policy, led to a revised approach to development. Structural change emerged strongly through the emphasis on institutional autonomy and the delegation of financial and educational authority to individual schools in a climate of decentralisation and marketisation. The view of organisational and structural change as the path to reform led to the introduction of Local Management of Schools (LMS) in the 1988 Education Reform Act, the incorporation of colleges post-1992, the establishment of Training and Enterprise Councils (TECs), and the Further Education Funding Council (FEFC) (later replaced by local Learning and Skills Councils (LSCs) and the national LSC). As a result the organisational chart of 14–19 education and training was radically restructured, with LEAs losing most of their role, and individual schools and colleges having to assume the challenges of self-management, autonomy and enhanced accountability.

Wave 3 – curriculum change

The third wave of curriculum change has a longer periodicity than the first two waves, and a number of minor crests and troughs. It began with the evolution of National Vocational Qualifications (NVQs) in the 1980s under the auspices of Gilbert Jessup and the National Council for Vocational Qualifications (NCVQ), and the establishment of GCSE by 1986. Post-1990, the rhetoric of integrating vocational and academic curricula for 14–19 year olds has been a strong theme. GNVQs (General National Vocational Qualifications) were established to provide a bridge between academic and vocational pathways, and the Qualifications and Curriculum Authority (QCA) was established to provide an integrated curriculum body. The introduction of *Curriculum 2000* brought together academic and vocational qualifications for the first time into a single framework, while retaining the centrality of A levels. Most recently, the belated implementation of the general proposals of the Tomlinson Report in the form of new specialised diplomas for 14–19 year olds over the period 2006–2010, has continued the emphasis on curriculum reform as the key tool for implementing policy development (DfES 2005a).

The story of waves of change is a convincing one, and emphasises the sequential impact of different strategies and approaches. But although the surface turbulence is unequivocally clear, how far is the change it describes real and persistent? The narrative of change has two forms: the narrative that evolves through the direct subjective experiences of those involved; and the narrative that can be seen in retrospect by a more objective analysis in the context of larger-scale changes. The two narratives may coincide, and in the context of 14–19 any analysis will identify the intensity (e.g. the rise and fall of GNVQs), the contradictions (e.g. the constraint of choice by marketisation), the conflict (e.g. between schools and colleges in competing for 16-year-old students) and the confusion in the system. Alternatively, the narratives may not coincide, and from our analysis we contend that it is simply myth to assert that 14–19 has been characterised by radical and continuous change which has produced a fundamentally different landscape for young people and for those working in the sector.

Change has two distinctive elements. At a superficial level change is a state in which 'the way things are done' is modified, on timescales ranging from days to years. Systems and processes are altered in response to evolutionary change resulting from evaluation and striving for improvement. Alternatively, they may alter by stepwise change when a new way of doing things is introduced by legislation or by professional authority. Changing the way things are done, however, does not necessarily change either the ultimate outputs of the system or the underlying principles that characterise the sector. These principles lie in the cultural and professional values and the societal expectations that underpin the system at the macro scale. Where these canons of culture remain unmodified, or are reinforced rather than reconstructed, then we might assert that, for all the surface activity and turbulence in the system, the reality is that significant change has not occurred.

This is clearly the case in relation to, for example, the 14–19 curriculum, which retains its strong academic basis, its emphasis on knowledge-based pathways to higher education and the lower social and market value accorded to vocational pathways. The steady growth in the value of vocational pathways has been a strongly espoused political aim of successive governments, yet it is equally clear that this has not been achieved, and that the rhetoric reflects a political ideal of change that has insufficient force and momentum to overcome strong resistance to the notion across much of society.

We would also question a key touchstone of the educational narrative – that there has been fundamental change in participation in learning and training among young people in the 16–19 age group, attributed by each of the key stakeholders in education (government and professionals) to their own vision, policy and practice. Concern about the low level of participation of young people post-16 has been a consistent theme of government policy since the late 1970s, and the most recent strategies for 14–19 (DfES 2005b) seek to raise post-16 participation rates from 75 per cent in 2005 to 90 per cent by 2010. The drive to increase participation so far, though, appears to have led to only relatively small increases in the numbers in education or training, but a shift in the pattern of what they do. Payne (2001) shows, using data from the England and Wales Youth Cohort Study (YCS), that in 1989 48 per cent of 16/17 year olds were in full-time education, with 24 per cent in some form of work base-related training and 23 per cent in full-time jobs. By 2002, 71 per cent were in full-time education, only 9 per cent in work base-related training and 9 per cent in full-time employment. As Payne indicates:

> Thus the rise in participation in full-time education did not represent a sudden upsurge of interest in qualifications and skill development, but rather a shift in its location from the workplace to the classroom.
>
> (Payne 2001: 4)

Policy process or policy learning?

Frequent, short-term policy change as described here is a well-established phenomenon at a global scale. It results partly from the political necessity for government to be seen to be doing something to address current socio-economic issues, and to be doing something different from (and hence by implication better than) political predecessors. Moreover, such necessity requires tangible evidence of achievement on the timescale of electoral cycles rather than on the timescales of educational processes. Policy change is of course also a response to the changing external environment, and is normally explained in terms of sustaining or enhancing global economic competitiveness, reflecting political pragmatism and economic instrumentalism. However, there are numerous frames for making sense of policy-making and policy learning. An apparently rational approach predicated on clear goals and a logical response to economic and social need can be interpreted quite differently. For example, the process can be seen as political rather than rational, essentially concerned with maintaining or adjusting the power differential between groups. Whatever its motivation, and however the process is interpreted, the ubiquitous short-term change must be seen as seeking an instant adjustment of the course in the turbulent global political/economic ocean.

But given that policy change is so rapid, why has it remained a touch on the tiller rather than a re-plotting of the course? Why has there been so little change in fundamental direction in 14–19 education? Our analysis suggests that education is a field of conflict, defined as: 'a situation in which interdependent people express (manifest or latent) differences in satisfying their individual needs and interests, and they experience interference from each other in accomplishing these goals' (Donohue and Kolt 1992: 4).

The 'interference' is experienced by a range of interdependent groups, the least powerful of which is learners. The education outputs and outcomes preferred by government, employers, parents, individual learners and educators differ considerably (Lumby and Foskett 2005), and so the achievement of the goals of one group is impeded by the achievement of the goals of one or more others. As a result, policy will inevitably be greeted by a curmudgeonly response, seen as a failure by one or more groups at any time, often interpreted by the disappointed individual or group as a failure of policy-makers to 'learn'.

Analysis of policy learning generally focuses on the process of policy change, not on the underlying process of learning. The sophistication of theory, which is utilised to better understand learning in other contexts, is not applied in relation to the learning of policy-makers. Generally, analysis of learning usually assumes a starting point of supporting the learner to achieve agreed goals. Commentary on the learning of policy-makers seems to reverse this stance and is generally evaluated by how far it achieves results that meet the goals of others, those affected by or wishing to influence policy decisions. The assumed 'failure to learn' is indicated as evident by other people's judgement that mistakes are being repeated. The policy-maker may of course feel quite differently, that they have learned very well, but their criteria of judgement may be different. The learning of individual policy-makers and groups of policy-makers has not been subject to the rigorous testing of learning theory. Are existing theories of adult learning appropriate or do we need alternative models, not only to comprehend the learning processes of policy-makers, but to better understand how it might be supported? In the remainder of the chapter, two alternative frames for exploring learning are applied to policy-makers as illustrations of how we might begin to explore, not the process of policy-making and policy change, but the individual learning which underlies it.

Policy learning

Gaming

Gaming theory, a branch of mathematics originally developed in relation to economics, has been annexed by behavioural and social scientists and provides a particular perspective on learning (Gantt and Reber 1999). The theory assumes that in any situation, individuals are players who make choices and develop strategies to accrue the greatest advantage to themselves. Over time they develop an understanding of the probable consequences of specific strategies through assessing the results of previous choices. They may also be able to predict the behaviour of others with whom they have competed, and such predictions too will affect strategy. The theory suggests that individuals will generally make rational decisions based on a calculation related to the greatest gain/smallest loss, but they may also act irrationally, for example in revenge to rob others of a reward, even at their own cost. Gaming is ubiquitous in humans and inherent even in lower forms of life. 'Even social bacteria have evolved optimal strategies for stabbing each other in the back' (Sapolsky 2002: 1). The results of experiments on how players make choices offer rich and challenging insights into the behaviour of human beings, and particularly into how they learn. If this theory of learning were applied to policy-makers, would it offer any useful insights into their process of learning?

First, this theory frames the purpose of learning in a particular way and would assume policy-makers are not using learning in a liberal sense to enlarge their understanding, increase their social skills, their capacity to contribute to humanity etc. Rather, learning is about individual gain. Players can act co-operatively to achieve gains for a number of individuals and may even accept some degree of loss if the game plan is, thereby, ultimately to gain. The theory, therefore, challenges the notion that policy learning is intended to achieve gains for society at large. The overt intention to act to your own benefit is generally not perceived as acceptable in a public policy arena; hence discussion about educational policy is couched in different terms. Ochbuki and Suzuki (2003) draw on the work of Druckman (1994) and Harinck *et al.* (2000) to suggest three kinds of conflict issues:

Gain/loss issues – the acquisition or loss of resource
Correct/incorrect issues – differences of opinion on how a task should be performed
Right/wrong issues – Difference of opinion on underlying values.

Adapted from Ochbuki and Suzuki (2003: 63)

The gain/loss issues which gaming theory suggests drives learning are likely to be concealed by discussion of correct/incorrect and right/wrong issues. Gaming theory as a frame for understanding policy learning therefore suggests that while policy decisions will be underpinned habitually by calculations of potential gain or loss, the discourse will be disguised. The three waves of change outlined earlier in the chapter have been largely an expression of correct/incorrect adjustments, reflecting changes in tactics about the where and what of 14–19 education. Issues of right/wrong, that is the underlying values about the outcomes of education, its function in classifying the future of individuals, its adherence to the millennia-old primacy of the academic and the middle/upper class, are untouched. Policy has reflected experimentation with correct/incorrect tactics while offering persiflage for the lack of change in relation to the right/wrong issues which are driven by powerful groups' calculations of gain/loss. The underlying calculations appear not to have varied much in the last three decades.

Much government rhetoric implies the goal is changing the culture, that is that policy is predicated on right/wrong issues, for example, the persistent theme that vocational pathways should be valued as much as academic. Trompenaars and Woolliams (2003) argue that cultures act to protect their own existence and that 'the reason for changing certain aspects is to avoid changing other aspects'. It is relatively easy to devise new strategies to change the surface processes of education, and such busyness may act to conceal the underlying assessment of gain/loss and the resulting absence of movement in relation to right/wrong issues. Such change can be understood not so much as a deep process of cumulatively adjusting beliefs and values, and, as a result, policy, but rather as gaming. The interplay of calculations of the gain or loss made at individual, sub-unit (school, college, Regional Development Agency) and government level will drive decisions about change, or in the case of 14–19 education, has maintained, despite all the appearance of turbulence, a steady state. The leverage for change, therefore, lies not with encouragement for policy learning in a conventional sense, that is assessing education effects and adjusting in response, but rather through the kind of learning embedded in gaming. Individuals and groups will make calculations as to their best strategy to maintain their position or to gain. Judgements about the likely actions of others will influence strategy, including whether to co-operate, or to act deliberately, overtly or covertly, to gain advantage or to undermine or disadvantage others (Kelly 2003).

The leverage for change in this perspective lies with encouraging learning about how gain and loss might be differently calculated, but the suggestions offered by gaming theory present real difficulties to researchers and practitioners. Mutual altruism can be encouraged between erstwhile competitors when there are multiple iterations of the game, such that players have time to learn about the game plan and the habitual strategies of others. One key consideration therefore is timescale. Policy-makers must be in post sufficiently long for the game strategies of players to be experienced and understood. If players are to tolerate short-term loss for long-term gain, then the degree of advantage to different groups of various strategies must be outlined, rather than the habitual analysis of advantage just to learners, or to the economy. A wider analysis of the predicted outcomes of strategies is provided by political analysts and advisers, usually in private. Researchers will continue to be assessed as of relatively little use in evolving game strategy if they present rational evidence in a way which does not relate to the rewards sought by policy-makers; such rewards relate to individual and party interests at least as much as those of learners or society. Such practice challenges the apolitical, rational stance of researchers. Gaming theory, therefore, presents no silver bullet to support policy learning, but points the way to the necessity to educate policy-makers in minimum losses as well as maximum gains resulting from policy choices with both short-term and long-term perspectives.

Espoused theory and theory-in-use

Any theoretical framework will impel a particular perspective and obscure the possibilities introduced by alternative theories. Gaming theory might be critiqued as being too narrow, pessimistic and mechanistic in its assessment of human behaviour. It might, therefore, be useful to explore a second illustration of how a theory of learning might elucidate policy learning.

Adopting an alternative frame, we might explore the relevance of another seminal framework for understanding adult learning, Argyris' (1991) analysis of how and why highly competent professional people learn in ways which, as with gaming theory, are different to liberal notions of the nature and purpose of learning. Argyris suggests that habitually defensive behaviour relates to an unwillingness to acknowledge and confront one's own errors or weakness. The result is a propensity to blame factors other than one's own behaviour and choices for unsatisfactory outcomes. Over time, a mythological self-image emerges based on 'espoused theory' (p. 103), which is perceived by others as in contradiction to 'theory-in-use', the reality as perceived by others. How might such theory apply to the learning of policy-makers, and in particular, policy-makers at national level? Argyris' theory is founded on the unwillingness of professionals in organisations to deal with the possibility of their own mistakes and weaknesses because of the compulsion to maintain a positive self-image. Learning occurs, but it is focused on how to maintain self-image, not how to achieve rational change. Policy learning at national, regional and local levels may be shaped by similar individual compulsion, but added to this is the political imperative generally to present a relentlessly positive perspective and only rarely, and for carefully calculated reasons, to admit error. It would seem to be implied that the nature of learning and the gulf between espoused theory and theory-in-action are likely to be greater for policy-makers than for those taking decisions in a more limited professional sphere.

Argyris focuses on changing the nature of learning, quoted here in an interview with Crossman (2003: 41):

> Human beings are skilful at two kinds of reasoning. One I call productive reasoning and the other I call defensive reasoning. Now, the function of productive reasoning is to seek, as best we can, truth about the effectiveness of what we do and what we claim. This gives rise to causality, testing, the notion of transparency, testing methodology, and so on. Defensive reasoning, serving as self-protection, leads to self-referential logic.

Argyris believes that techniques can aid individuals to become self-critical and metamorphose their learning. Specifically, they can be supported to move from single-loop learning, that is a reactive process of adjustment to achieve goals which are unquestioned, to double-loop learning, where the way the questions and goals are conceived is challenged. They can be supported to move from adjustment to transformation. The espoused theory of national policy makers is evident in national documents and legislation. For example, the White Paper, *14–19 Education and Skills* (2005b: 5) states 'Our aim is to transform secondary and post-secondary education'. The analysis in the first part of this chapter suggests that rather than transformation, a steady state disguised by the busyness of superficial change has been the intention, the theory-in-use. In order for policy-makers to learn, Argyris' (1991: 100) theory suggests that they must 'learn how the very way they go about defining and solving problems can be a source of problems in its own right'. In other words, the discourse centred on correct/incorrect issues, that is, single-loop learning, must be shifted to a discourse of right/wrong issues, double-loop learning.

This theoretical frame suggests strongly that the most frequent method of trying to achieve this shift, the presentation of rational evidence related to the 'failure' of policy, or to negative unintended effects, is likely only to embed ever more strongly defensive behaviour and an inability to learn. Adopting such a perspective on the learning of policy-makers leads to the conclusion that the rational efforts of those attempting to influence policy-makers, for example researchers, seem perfectly designed to contribute to strengthening a system which resists change other than at a superficial level. Researchers may, therefore, be unconsciously complicit in the maintenance of single-loop learning.

The theory of organisational learning is generally more compelling on the pressures which lead to single-loop learning than on the intervention strategies which might transform it. Intervention to encourage honest self-reflection about the differences between espoused theory and theory-in-use is a potentially painful process which most professionals and policy-makers are skilled at avoiding (Argryis 1991). There is relatively little that is concrete to guide those who wish to make such an intervention. Argyris points out that there has been little research on double-loop learning (Crossman 2003). Such a view points us firmly back to the necessity for those who wish to influence policy learning to focus as much on the learning as on the policy. Rather than repeated evaluation of the latest policy and its effects, more effort is perhaps needed to research how the defensive and self-referential learning which currently dominates the policy-making arena could be challenged and transformed.

Future directions

The chapter has reviewed 14–19 policy over the last three decades and concluded that it has resulted in turbulence at the surface and not fundamental change. Rather than attributing this to a failure of policy learning, it has suggested the necessity to apply deeper analysis, not to policy learning but to the learning of individual policy-makers. Policies don't learn and make choices. People do. Only two frameworks for learning have been briefly considered, but each suggests quite different insights into how policy decisions are reached, how learning results during the process and how such learning could be influenced. There are of course many other theories which could be usefully mined for further insights. For example, the theory of adults as learners would suggest that the characteristics and career point of the individual policy-maker may be relevant (Cross 1981). Equally, is gender relevant to the learning of policy-makers? Do novices learn in a similar or different way to seasoned politicians? It may be that a theory of policy learning is needed if we are to move from bewailing a failure to learn to understanding better how to support it.

References

Argyris, C. (1991) 'Teaching smart people how to learn'. *Harvard Business Review*, May–June, 99–109.

Cross, K.P. (1981) *Adults as Learners*. San Frasncisco: Jossey-Bass.

Crossman, M. (2003) 'Altering theories of learning and action: an interview with Chris Argyris'. *Academy of Management Executive*, 17 (2), 40–6.

Department for Education and Skills (DfES) (2005a) *The 14–19 Implementation Plan*. London: DfES.

— (2005b) *14–19 Education and Skills*. London: HMSO.

Donohue, W.A. and Kolt, R. (1992) *Managing Interpersonal Conflict*. Newbury Park: Sage.

Druckman, D. (1994) 'Determinants of compromising behaviour in negotiation'. *Journal of Conflict Resolution*, 38 (3), 507–56.

Gantt, E. and Reber, J. (1999) 'Sociobiological and social constructionist accounts of altruism: a phenomenological critique'. *Journal of Phenomenological Psychology* , 30 (2). Online. Available HTTP: http://search.epnet.com/direct.asp?an=2930785&db=afh (accessed 13 September 2006).

Goulding, J., Dominey, J. and Gray, M. (1998) *Hard Nosed Decisions: Planning human resources in FE*. London: Further Education Development Agency (FEDA).

Harinck, F., De Dreu, C. and Vianen, A. (2000) 'The impact of conflict issues on fixed-pie perceptions, problem-solving and integrative outcomes in negotiation'. *Organizational Behaviour and Human Decision Processes*, 81 (2), 329–58.

Kelly, A.J. (2003) *Decision-making and Game Theory*. Cambridge: Cambridge University Press.

Lumby, J. and Foskett, N. (2005) *14–19 Education: Policy, leadership and learning*. London: Paul Chapman.

Ochbuki, K. and Suzuki, M. (2003) 'Three dimensions of conflict issues and their effects on resolution strategies in organizational settings'. *International Journal of Conflict Management*, 14 (1), 61–73.

Payne, J. (2001) *Patterns of Participation in Full-time Education after 16: An analysis of the England and Wales Youth Cohort Study*. London: DfES.

Salter, B. and Tapper, T. (eds) (1981) *Education, Politics and the State: The theory and practice of educational change*. London: Grant McIntyre.

Sapolsky, R. (2002) 'Cheaters and chumps: game theorists offer a surprising insight into the evolution of fair play – findings'. *Natural History*, June. Online. Available HTTP: http://www.findarticles.com/p/articles/mi--_m1134/is_5_111/ai_86684497 (accessed 22 August 2004).

Trompenaars, F. and Woolliams, P. (2003) 'A new framework for managing change across cultures'. *Journal of Change Management*, 3 (4), 361–75.

5 Policy continuity and policy learning in the *Action Plan, Higher Still* and beyond

John Hart and Ron Tuck

This chapter explores some of the factors that have affected policy-making in education for 14–19 year olds in Scotland over the past 30 years. It does so by examining three important periods of educational policy-making: those centred on the publication by the Scottish Office of: *16–18s in Scotland: An action plan* – commonly referred to as *Action Plan* (SED 1983); *Higher Still: Opportunity for all* – commonly referred to as *Higher Still* (SOED 1994); and *A Curriculum for Excellence* (SEED 2004a, b).

In this study the authors have taken the term 'policy learning' to refer to a process where policy-makers take full and conscious account of the successes and failures of earlier policies relevant to the area in which they are working. The policy learning may vary in formality, range of reference and scope, and the result could be the adoption, amendment or rejection of specific ideas or approaches. Information gathering about policies and their effects may be more or less systematic: for example, it might involve methodical and dedicated monitoring and evaluation of policy implementation or it might mean deriving indications of the effectiveness of specific aspects of policy implementation from data which are already generated for other purposes. The field of reference could range from widely-based international studies, to selective or regional studies (e.g. in the case of Scotland, studies confined to Anglophone countries or to EU countries), to the examination of domestic policies. And the scope of policy learning may be broad and strategic, or it may be more narrowly focused, concerning itself with specific, practical issues. Evidence of almost all of these kinds of policy learning appears in Scotland at different times in the period discussed, but there is no evidence of consistent or systematic approaches to policy learning. We believe that there are a number of reasons for this.

First, the most innovative and significant policy developments may not be worked out in detail, meaning that policy-making and implementation are not entirely sequential. This means that, while a model of *policy-making → implementing → reviewing → drawing lessons → fresh policy-making based on policy learning* undoubtedly applies to some extent and in some circumstances, practice is more likely to be less systematic than the model might suggest. In the case of *Higher Still*, for example, a deliberate attempt was made to ensure that development should be responsive to feedback through practical modelling and wide-scale consultation and, in that sense, the development of policy within the framework set by the initial publication was deliberately based on new evidence rather than a study of past issues.

Secondly, the speed at which policy development is required (by politicians) or expected (by stakeholders) to proceed often rules out the serious examination and evaluation of previous policy. In the case of *Action Plan*, changes were initiated to deal with immediate and growing economic problems and there was an expectation that, if the principles of *Action Plan* were beneficial to young people looking for worthwhile vocational pathways, they should quickly be extended to other learners and potential learners. Political pressures and stakeholder expectations were such that it was difficult to gather firm enough or clear enough data on the implementation of any stage of the initiative to guide the next stage. The result was that, while there were some studies of the impact of the reforms, they were mainly taken forward on the basis of piloting and action research. In other words meeting political requirements and stakeholder expectations is likely to focus learning more on how to implement than on the results of implementation.

Thirdly, there is an issue about the coverage and complexity of different policy developments and the extent to which these affect the value of lessons that can be learned. In particular, we shall see that while the predecessor initiatives to *Higher Still* were limited in scope, *Higher Still* was relatively comprehensive – bringing together general and vocational education and covering the curriculum, subject syllabuses, assessment systems and processes, and qualifications structure. This made it more much complex than the developments which had preceded it and this added complexity appears to have negated attempts to apply lessons from the earlier initiatives.

Fourthly, comparisons made between national systems with a view to policy learning will always have to be undertaken cautiously, since the factors which influence success and failure will vary greatly. These will include the geographic, demographic, economic and cultural backgrounds. Even within the UK, differences in all of these factors are considerable and, within the period covered by this chapter, Scottish policy-makers have been more concerned with establishing systems which respond to the traditions and expectations of the nation as with learning from the other jurisdictions. A current example of this would be the way in which the National Debate on Education, which preceded *A Curriculum for Excellence*, made clear that Scottish stakeholders continued to support the system of comprehensive schools, creating a significant cross-border policy difference within the UK, which must greatly lessen the scope for valid comparisons and policy learning.

In the case of Scottish policy-making in the field of 14–19 vocational education, it is also true that, since the 1990s, Scotland has been seen internationally as a leader in many of the aspects of education and training that this chapter covers. This has meant that Scottish policy-makers have often been more engaged in offering, than in seeking, policy advice and may therefore have been less inclined to look at other, differently based, systems. The kind of advisory role which other countries gave Scottish policy-makers can, of course, also give the opportunity for informal policy learning – through feedback on the development and implementation of policy which draws on the Scottish approach – but no specific evidence of this kind of policy learning emerged from our study.

Finally, comparisons across time with a view to policy learning will be affected by changes in economic and political circumstances and these may make comparisons unhelpful. In the case of Scotland, the period covered not only includes a difficult economic period, when policy-making was being carried out under a government formed by a minority party in Scotland, but also the establishment of the Scottish Parliament and a consequent significant shift in power and influence within the policy community. The authors argue that the latter change has meant that the policy-making process has changed to an extent which must make policy learning difficult – perhaps impossible – until the new political dispensation is fully established and valid comparisons between policy initiatives can be made.

What emerges most clearly from the Scottish experience – certainly during the 1990s – is evidence of an expectation that policy development should be incremental. Arguably, an incremental approach must involve at least a measure of continuous review and learning. However, although there is some evidence that most stages in the development of policy across the 30 years has been shaped to some extent by the perceived successes and failures of previous stages, it also appears that some policies are simply repeated without account being taken of what had happened previously. In this study, we are only able to note the questions which this raises: does it happen because of a lack of firm evidence about the effectiveness of the previous policies? Or does it happen because policy-makers judge that the policy context is so changed that no worthwhile lessons can be drawn from the past?

Note on age structures

It is perhaps worth noting right away that the term '14–19' does not have the significance in Scotland that it appears to have in other parts of the UK and that this itself, in the form of a debate about the appropriateness of 'age and stage' regulations has been a policy issue throughout the period. In Scotland attention is more likely to be focused on 14–18 year olds or 16–18 year olds and the emphasis is most likely to be on those following courses in school – for most of the period, the majority of 16–18 year olds. However, it is also true that, in terms of qualifications at least, no systematic distinction is made in Scotland between provision for young people and provision for adults.

Of the three initiatives dealt with here, the first started as the *16–18 Action Plan*, but quickly became referred to as the *16-plus Action Plan* and then simply *Action Plan*. In making this change policy-makers were including all post-compulsory learners, without age limit. The move to an outcomes-based qualifications system which was at the heart of *Action Plan* seemed logically to lead in this direction and to rule out distinctions based on the age of the learner or the place of learning – an innovation in policy terms. In addition, and driven largely by the need for new provision to meet the requirements of the Technical and Vocational Education Initiative (TVEI) in schools, *Action Plan* provision was also used with 14–16 year olds. Since the provision which was developed by the *Action Plan* was modular and led to externally moderated internal assessment, this did not challenge the existing regulations on presentation for national examinations, which set a minimum age for entry. There was some pressure to extend the use of modules in areas such as computing back to the first two years of secondary schooling (i.e. 12–14 year olds), but this was resisted on the basis that the qualifications were intended to have a vocational use and there was no obvious value – either for students or employers – in formally recording these early achievements. From this time, however, concerns about the validity of restricting access to qualifications solely on the basis of the age of the learners has been an important strand in qualifications policy.

The second policy initiative discussed in this chapter, *Higher Still*, was preceded by the establishment of a committee to examine the fifth and sixth years of Scottish secondary schooling (i.e. provision for 16–18 year olds). The committee, under the chairmanship of John Howie, carried out its work between 1990 and 1992. The fact that the committee's remit was restricted in this way suggests a lack of policy learning about the need for a more inclusive approach – an impression which is supported by the fact that the committee found it impossible to fulfil their remit without making recommendations which affected both 14–16 year olds and students older than 18. Since the majority of young people were staying on in school beyond 16, argued the committee, it no longer made sense to pivot so much on a formal leaving examination at the end of the fourth, final compulsory, year. And since many young Scots were taking the main post-compulsory qualifications – Scottish Certificate of Education Higher Grade courses, known as 'Highers' – after one year (i.e. at the end of the fifth year), the need to prepare for end-of-session examinations in the fourth year had the negative effect of creating a very pressurised fifth year – the so-called 'two-term dash' to prepare for Highers. The Howie Committee proposed new certificates which would start in the fourth year and continue into post-compulsory education, which might mean further education (FE) colleges. In effect this meant that the committee was making recommendations which would affect both pre-16s and post-18s and so went beyond their original remit. The specific proposals were rejected and as a result, the remit for *Higher Still* was stated cautiously but still managed to acknowledge what both *Action Plan* and the Howie Committee had demonstrated about the interrelatedness of the different educational stages. 'Ministers,' it stated:

> have decided that some changes are required to courses and
> qualifications in the upper stages of Scottish secondary education.
> The changes will also affect some of the courses and qualifications
> offered in further education colleges and, to a limited extent, the
> arrangements in S1 to S4.
>
> (SOED 1994: 6.1)

The cautious tone was appropriate because the extent to which the provision developed under *Higher Still* could be used with students younger than 16, was governed by the Executive's 'age and stage' regulations. However, since the introduction of the 'new National Qualifications' developed by the Higher Still Development Programme, the Scottish Executive has twice consulted on these regulations. The first consultation, in 1998, led to the lowering of the age at which students could take national examinations by one year and advice to local authorities to review their current approaches to flexibility and innovation in the curriculum (SEED 2001a).

The second consultation, in 2004, led to the complete replacement of the regulations by guidelines for schools and local authorities, a decision which was highlighted in the ministerial response to the third reforming document being considered here – *A Curriculum for Excellence*, which sets principles for curricula for children and young people from 3–18. It is not directly concerned with learners in colleges, although it will bring schools and colleges together through new Skills for Work courses intended primarily for 14–16 year old students, but also available for 16–18 year olds.

Munn, Dunning and *Action Plan*

Following the raising of the school leaving age in the early 1970s, two committees – named for their Chairmen, the Munn and Dunning Committees – were established to review, respectively, the curriculum and assessment/certification for the new final years of compulsory education. Both committees proposed radical changes, and their ideas were brought together by the then Scottish Education Department (SED), introducing new Standard Grade courses designed to be available to all students aged 14–16, regardless of academic ability. These courses were to use criterion-referenced internal and external assessment for certification. The popularity of Standard Grades led to a review of Highers taken by 17 and 18 year olds and some adults. Criterion-referenced assessment – which was known to be in use in some parts of the USA and Canada – was used in these revised courses. The Munn Report (SED 1977) also proposed the development of short courses, but this aspect of the report was not immediately acted upon, nor does it appear to be the origin of the later modular approach adopted by the *Action Plan*. All of these courses were awarded by the Scottish Certificate of Education Examinations Board (SCEEB), later the Scottish Examinations Board (SEB).

Action Plan also employed criterion-referenced assessment in a radical reform of post-compulsory general and vocational provision. The timing of these developments makes it hard to see whether there was any sequential policy learning in this case. However, shared leadership, centred on Her Majesty's Inspectorate of Schools, ensured that certain ideas were common to the different developments and there is some evidence of what might be called pragmatic policy learning. For example, in its early phase, Standard Grade required a form of local peer moderation of provision, but this was difficult for local authorities to resource and was soon dropped: similar mechanisms were encouraged, but not required, for the later *Action Plan* implementation.

The SED published *16–18s in Scotland: An action plan* in January 1983. In format it was a very modest document, the title simply indicated the intended scope of the paper, and the introduction was very matter of fact. The contents, however, with their proposals to introduce a new unitised provision for post-16s, were revolutionary and set the direction of policy for at least the next 20 years. The opening paragraphs referred back to a 1979 consultative paper, *16–18s in Scotland: The first two years of post-compulsory education* (SED 1979). The issues that had been consulted on were listed, and the responses to the consultation were dealt with very briefly, as follows:

> The paper was well received and the responses reflected a desire for reform. They did not, however, reveal any consensus of opinion on the changes which were necessary to make better and more co-ordinated provision for the age group. Nevertheless, some of the ideas canvassed in the paper attracted sufficient support to justify further work on new post-16 courses with a more pronounced vocational emphasis; closer co-operation between schools and further education colleges; and changes in the structure of post-school education.
>
> (SED 1983: 1.3)

It went on to state that the 'further work' was to take two forms: a new Certificate in Vocational Studies (CVS) being developed by the Scottish Technical Education Council (SCOTEC) and the Scottish Business Education Council (SCOTBEC) – shortly to be merged to become the Scottish Vocational Education Council (SCOTVEC); and an agreement by the General Teaching Council (GTC) that FE lecturers could teach 16–18 year olds in school in 'certain circumstances'. The new certificate encouraged collaboration between schools and FE colleges. In the event, the new certificate was short-lived.

Over the years since 1979 a number of attempts have been made to create awards like the CVS, and some of these are discussed in this chapter. A number of attempts have also been made to increase the links between schools and colleges and at the time of writing, the Scottish Executive intends to make vocational courses available to all school students in FE colleges in the next few years – the Skills for Work courses, referred to above. However, at the time of writing the circumstances under which FE lecturers can work with school-age students is still a matter of debate. Does this mean that policy lessons have not been learned? When one considers the many changes that have taken place in the policy environment, it is easy to see why resolving the issue of cross-sector teaching in school–college links has not been a priority and has not been resolved. In 1979, for example, FE colleges came under the control of local authorities and were not encouraged to innovate or expand; at the same time, schools had just begun to implement curricula which did not divide the academic from the vocational and were cautious about moves towards more vocational provision. Today schools are willingly exploring the role of vocational learning, but the colleges are incorporated bodies encouraged to adopt business practices to extend their provision and take on new clients. Thus, it could be argued, what in 1979 might have been primarily an issue for schools about how they perceived the capability of the FE staff who were to engage with their pupils and about the quality of the experience these pupils might have, has become an issue for colleges about how they perceive the requirements of the GTC and the effects which meeting these requirements might have on their ethos and their ability to fulfil their wider missions. In these circumstances it seems unlikely that a study of the policy issues as they were understood and addressed in 1979 would aid policy-makers in 2006.

The planning and implementation of the Scottish *Action Plan* took place in a period when training policy was created by UK ministries and education policy was being shaped by an unpopular and unrepresentative Conservative Scottish administration. It was also a time when unemployment, including youth unemployment, was growing, and there was an urgent need to develop a workforce with new technological and transferable skills. The UK's Manpower Services Commission (MSC) had a lead role in developing and implementing policy for the UK in respect of these concerns, particularly through youth training schemes and the TVEI. *Action Plan* also took some lessons from thinking beyond Scotland – notably from American developments in competence-based learning and assessment – but it is often hard to determine how much of the policy learning was specifically Scottish and how much was filtered through the policy development processes of the MSC.

The work of the MSC in Scotland had come under the Secretary of State for Scotland since July 1977, but it was still very heavily influenced from England. Also initiatives such as the Review of Vocational Qualifications and the Modular Accreditation Development (MAD) Programme – which would lead to the development of National and Scottish Vocational Qualifications (NVQs and SVQs) and the establishment of the National Council for Vocational Qualifications (NCVQ) – threatened the independence of Scottish policies and approaches. Any learning from UK policy in Scotland, therefore, was heavily dominated by the need to find ways to maintain the distinctiveness of the Scottish system while meeting government policy. Thus the work of the MSC is referred to in the introduction to *Action Plan*, but only to make it clear that Scotland would be going its own way, using the new Standard Grade courses for 14–16s and *Action Plan* itself.

Action Plan implementation was not without its critics, but was largely accepted for its benefits, particularly in increasing flexibility in the curriculum. The numbers of candidates registered for the National Certificate modules which it introduced more than doubled in the first five years of the system and the number of modules they were taking rose even more dramatically. These advantages were so immediately apparent that within five years work had started on the unitisation of Higher National Certificates and Diplomas (HNCs and HNDs), following consultation, but driven by the demands of the college sector. Was this an example of policy learning? Again the answer depends on an analysis of the policy environment. It is true that the approach which was taken to the unitisation of Higher National qualifications could be seen as addressing some of the issues raised by *Action Plan* implementation, with more attention being paid, for example, to staff development and issues of quality assurance. However, many of the novelties of approach (particularly the extent to which responsibilities in the new provision were devolved to the colleges working with sectoral stakeholders to increase ownership and maximise flexibility) owe as much to pragmatism in the face of the expressed views of parts of the college sector as to any radical analysis of the implementation of *Action Plan* which was, after all, very recent.

It was noted in *Action Plan* that the proposals were not worked out in detail, but the paper set out the educational principles upon which action should be taken as well as saying who should be taking action and what action they should be taking. The introduction ended with the gnomic statement: 'This paper is ... not prescriptive, but neither is it simply part of a further consultative process' (SED 1983: 1.6). Within three years the entire FE vocational curriculum had been unitised and a wide range of new general modules for use in schools and colleges had been introduced. All of this was recorded on one, cumulative certificate to replace the qualifications offered by SCOTEC, SCOTBEC and City and Guilds London Institute (CGLI). However, as noted above, the promised joint vocational studies certificate was not part of the new framework and there was little or no interchange of staff between schools and colleges. This development work was carried out by groups of practitioners led by HMI. *Action Plan* brought the ideas of progression and articulation to the fore and laid the ground for more sophisticated credit transfer, starting a policy process which would lead in due course to the integration of vocational and academic courses through the Higher Still Development Programme, the formation of the Scottish Qualifications Authority (SQA), and the development of the Scottish Credit and Qualifications Framework. This process can be followed though a series of publications, consultations and initiatives based around the key concepts of opportunity and access.

Thus, although *Action Plan* was published and implemented at a time when education and training policy were driven by the economic concerns of the UK government, it can be argued that in policy terms the shape of *Action Plan* owes as much, or more, to the policy issues of the 1960s and 70s which were centred on the best ways to create a provision which would even out the chances of Scotland's young people within a common state system – a theme which would be picked up a decade later in *Higher Still* and which continues to dominate policy-making in the present day.

The Howie Committee and *Higher Still*

Higher Still: Opportunity for all was published by the Scottish Office Education Department (SOED) in March 1994 but, as indicated above, its significance in terms of the policy process can only be understood in the light of the report of the Howie Committee in 1992. In tracing the origins and development of *Higher Still*, serious attempts to learn from previous domestic initiatives and from international commentators can be identified. We can also see these being overruled on political grounds and negated by a misinterpretation of the views of stakeholders – particularly teachers – and also, perhaps by the very complexity of the reform.

The successes and failures of *Action Plan* in creating popular and useful short courses for 16–18 year olds was one of the factors which led to this major review. In the years following the raising of the leaving age, growing numbers of young people opted to remain at school for a further one or two years. However, while *Action Plan* allowed many to take programmes of practical, vocationally oriented modules awarded by SCOTVEC, many more felt that these courses lacked the credibility of more traditional academic provision and opted to take the traditional, academic Highers, which they were failing in large numbers. To address this, a review committee, chaired by Professor John Howie, previously a member of the Dunning Committee, was established by the Secretary of State for Scotland to review upper secondary education in Scotland (i.e. provision for 16–18 year olds). The secretariat of the Howie Committee was mainly drawn from inspectors with an *Action Plan* background.

The Howie Committee proposals were published by SOED in 1992 (SOED 1992). These proposals were intended to bring together the academic and vocational systems, but proposed a twin-track approach which would require Standard Grades to be moved back a year from S3–S4[1] (14–16 year olds) to S2–S3 (13–15 year olds) to allow students to start on programmes leading to new certificates. These were the Scotbac, achieved by a three-year academic track, and Scotcert, achieved by a one-or two-year vocational track. A majority of the 300 respondents to the report firmly rejected these proposals as divisive. It was generally felt that the two group awards were too different in content and structure to be held in equal regard and that the new arrangements would simply mirror the existing situation with a continuing high failure rate in individual component courses, and a poor completion rate in the new certificates. Consultees also rejected the associated proposal to move Standard Grade back a year.

Following this, there were two fallow years while the development of alternative proposals was undertaken within the Scottish Office, again led by the Inspectorate. The new policy proposals were drafted on the basis that support for many of the important features of the Howie Report could be assumed. Responses to Howie seemed to indicate that the committee's analysis of the issues and its intention of using national examinations coupled with internal assessment, of unitising all provision, and the continued use of the core skills which had been introduced by the White Paper *Access and Opportunity* (SOED 1991) were generally supported and needed no further debate. The result, *Higher Still: Opportunity for all* (SOED 1994), is a slim document, but in 12 of its 24 large print pages it set out the blueprint for radical changes to provision for all learners 14-plus. Politically it was a more important document than *Action Plan* since it had to recoup the ground lost by the failure of Howie and it would affect the future of the 100-year-old Highers, the university entrance qualification. It was introduced in a foreword by the Secretary of State and it had been through a process of clearance that closely involved UK as well as Scottish ministers.

In the course of development the *Higher Still* proposals had undergone significant change. In response to the critics of Howie's twin-track proposals, planners had developed a five-level group award structure said to be very similar to the Tomlinson proposals a decade later. However, just as the Tomlinson proposals were rejected by a Labour administration in favour of A levels in 2005, so, almost a decade earlier, these proposals were rejected by a Conservative administration in favour of Highers. Group awards, which came to be titled Scottish Group Awards (SGAs), did have a role in the proposals, but with a lower status than originally envisaged, and in the event these qualifications have not been successful.[2] Although this might be seen as a lesson learned from the Howie proposals, anecdotal evidence suggests that it was a political decision to avoid any changes which appeared to reduce the status of Highers. In the event, however, it may be that this was the right decision.

Were there lessons to be learned at the time of *Higher Still* from earlier developments of this kind? Certainly, as we have seen, the Certificate of Vocational Studies, which was proposed in *Action Plan* was never fully introduced and much of *Action Plan*'s success appeared to come from the freedom which was offered by a provision composed solely of individual units which could be combined into all sorts of programmes. On the other hand, once *Action Plan* was implemented colleges very quickly developed their own locally standardised National Certificate programmes – group awards in all but name – and successfully marketed their provision on the basis of these. General SVQs (GSVQs), introduced in 1992 on the basis of the requirements of *Access and Opportunity* (SOED 1991), were also increasingly being built into the college structure. In the school sector there was a similar tendency among schools which used modules in a coherent way, to want to group these into named programmes. GSVQs were used in some schools, but, designed primarily for delivery in colleges, they were difficult for most schools to resource and so Schools Group Awards (certificated with that title) were developed by SCOTVEC in collaboration with some local authorities. However, the tendency with academic qualifications was steadily to move away from any kind of fixed grouping of subjects such as the school leaving certificates and general entry requirements for university which can be found in the post-war years. In retrospect it might be considered that what came to be called a National Course – a 160-hour programme in a single subject area such as the Higher, bigger than a unit and smaller than a group certificate – was coherent enough for the purposes of school students.

The Higher Still Development Programme was launched before the establishment of a Scottish parliament, but was implemented by the first devolved administration – a Labour–Liberal alliance. *Higher Still: Opportunity for all* (SOED 1994) was described in briefings given by senior inspectors as 'a white paper with green edges' (cf. *Action Plan*, which was said to be neither prescriptive nor consultative) and policy-making within its overall structure was undertaken by a small number of committees with representatives of the main stakeholder organisations. Development work was undertaken by groups of subject experts from schools, colleges and relevant national organisations, remitted to bring together existing academic and vocational provision into a single unified set of units and courses at each of the levels set out in the policy document. This task was seen as relatively straightforward and the timescale for the reform was accordingly short.

Like the Howie Report, *Higher Still* was intended to lead to an all-encompassing reform which would address issues raised by the more piecemeal developments of the previous 20 years. Teachers and stakeholders should have welcomed this, but in the event there were difficulties in conveying the detailed scope of the proposals clearly to stakeholders. Also it may have been that some of the initial support for the areas of the Howie Report which were carried over to *Higher Still* had ebbed in the two years since that consultation. For many, perhaps most, stakeholders, the line of continuity from the Howie Report to *Higher Still* was not clear. Howie had reported after a process open to influence and Howie had been rejected; but after that it appeared that the policy-makers had gone into cabal and developed something that required a further debate which was not being held.

From the perspective of the policy-makers and those managing the development programme, the problem was that, because *Higher Still* was comprehensive it was complex. It was a challenge to ensure that those involved in development and implementation fully appreciated the consequences which a policy decision in one area might have on other areas – what might be called horizontal complexity as opposed to the vertical complexity of turning policy into action. To try to offset this, consultation on an industrial scale was carried out throughout the development programme. Consultations were held in the course of the Development Programme on most aspects of the emerging system, including post-16 curriculum principles, core skills and group awards, and draft subject documents were released for comment before being finalised. In spite of this, teachers felt that they were not sufficiently involved in the decision-making process, while those organisations which would be responsible for running the new system felt that too much attention had been paid to the concerns of subject experts and not enough to their concerns about implementation.

These negative results emerged against a background of policy learning. The planners in the Scottish Office were determined to ensure that this initiative would encourage and take account of feedback on the detail of the emerging system and that this should be gathered from real practitioners. In this they were influenced by both research and experience. In particular the work of the Canadian authority on educational reform, Michael Fullan, which emphasises the need to involve the schools and the teachers, was influential. However, they were also concerned to avoid two of the effects of Standard Grade, where the development of courses was left very firmly in the hands of practitioners, with a minimal input from the Scottish Certificate of Education Examinations Board (SCEEB, later the SEB). First, cascading, which was the means of dissemination for Standard Grade, was felt not to have worked effectively and therefore it was decided that staff development should be delivered directly by the programme. Secondly, the use of quasi-independent specialist groups of practitioner developers had resulted in the development of hugely burdensome assessment loads and led to an early review and revision of the Standard Grade courses to cut assessment back to manageable proportions. So to avoid this a strong central development team was established to ensure that the programme would be able to be implemented.

In the event, the process turned out to be different in a number of significant ways from what was planned, as teachers pursued their own agendas. First, where large groups of practitioners were brought together, the pace of the programme meant that demands for information and reassurance about details of the design – particularly as these affected specific subjects – were usually so insistent that views on larger-scale and more fundamental issues could not be gathered. Second, many practitioners wanted to challenge the basis of *Higher Still* and its link with Howie in ways which were not taken account of. Since there was no mechanism to allow this, negative views of the reforms could not be dealt with on a strategic level and this built up some resentment, which would surface very publicly when there were problems with implementation. Third, subject specialist groups were often unwilling or unable simply to bring together the two existing sets of provision and set out to undertake significant subject reforms of a kind that were not planned for. In some cases this was linked to the unresolved issues referred to above. One result was that many courses were created which, like Standard Grade before, were not practicable in assessment terms and had to be revised and slimmed down within two years of introduction.

The initial timescale for the programme was extended and the new national provision was introduced in August 1999 with the first certificates being issued in August 2000. Planners had proposed a number of school closure days for in-service training, but this was rejected by the Executive as politically unacceptable. As a result the programme was forced back into the cascade model discredited by Standard Grade and as a result most teachers did not understand the new certification regime and did not prepare pupils for it. This issue was exacerbated by a failure in the certification system in 2000.

The Scottish Qualifications Authority (SQA) was set up in 1997 by merging the SEB and SCOTVEC and it was given three years to create a fully integrated organisation operating a fully integrated system. This turned out to be overambitious. The data-gathering and data-processing systems were neither fully tested nor fully operational in 2000 and large numbers of unfortunate candidates received inaccurate certificates, creating turmoil in the national education system. It might be said that the high-profile difficulties experienced in introducing all-encompassing computing systems in other areas of public service might have offered lessons for policy-makers and suggested that the task the SQA was given was high risk and should not be rushed.

The certification failure threatened to precipitate a general crisis of confidence in the assessment system – the educational equivalent of a run on the banks – which required immediate and radical action. Among other measures taken to re-establish confidence, a National Qualifications Steering Group (NQSG) was established, with members drawn from key stakeholder organisations, and this group undertook a fundamental enquiry into the new system. Following that, as indicated above, an immediate and thorough review of new National Courses was put in train.

The NQSG drew on a wide range of evidence – including the results of the surveys conducted by stakeholder organisations such as the teacher unions, the Scottish Parent Teacher Council and the Scottish Further Education Unit. The report largely endorsed the original *Higher Still* policy document, making a clear distinction between the principles which governed the new system and the design features, which were the focus of most of the criticism. The NQSG found that the principles were founded in consultation and: 'recognised that the design features had not been arbitrarily determined but had been based on central features of the prior certification system and helped ensure the maintenance and development of a coherent qualifications system' (SEED 2001b: 2.16).

They also decided that these design features, which included unitisation and a balance of external and internal assessment, should be retained if possible, although it was clear that measures would be required to reduce the amount of assessment required in the new system.

Among the casualties of the debacle was the Inspectorate, which lost (for a time at least) its leading role in policy-making. However, it is arguable that the certification crisis of 2000 was the excuse, rather than the reason for the change in status of the Inspectorate. There are two reasons for thinking this. First, senior figures in educational management had publicly begun to challenge the multiform role of the Inspectorate in Scotland as makers, evaluators and enforcers of policy. Second, the initial years of *Higher Still* implementation had also been the first years of devolution; the main roles of the partly Westminster-based Secretary of State had been transferred to a fully home-based First Minister, and Scottish civil servants were getting used to an enhanced status within a new indigenous policy framework.

The National Debate on Education and *A Curriculum for Excellence*

In November 2004, the Scottish Executive published a handsome folder containing two complementary documents under the heading *A Curriculum for Excellence* (SEED 2004a, b). It contained the recommendations of a Curriculum Review Group established 12 months earlier and the ministerial response to the Group's proposals. The purpose of the review was to bring together 30 years of curriculum development and to create 'for the first time ever, a single curriculum 3–18, supported by a simple and effective structure of assessment and qualifications' (SEED 2004a: 4). These documents might also be seen as representing the emergence of post-devolution policy-making in education.

Tracing the route to *A Curriculum for Excellence* requires an examination of process as well as content and a digression to consider the role of cross-party committees in the devolved Parliament – in particular, the Education, Culture and Sport Committee (now the Education Committee) and the Enterprise and Lifelong Learning Committee (now the Enterprise and Culture Committee). In an early initiative the Enterprise and Lifelong Learning Committee conducted a national inquiry into lifelong learning which attracted much interest in the education and training community and beyond. Stakeholders showed an eagerness to participate in spite of the belief, current at the time, that the Higher Still Development Programme had left stakeholders suffering from 'consultation fatigue': 120 groups and individuals submitted evidence and 58 organisations offered oral evidence. The committee produced a well-received report in 2002, which ministers used as a basis for a policy paper a year later.

This was seen by many as a new start, heralding more consensual policy-making, but this now appears to have been a misapprehension. Not only does the role of cross-party committees seem less important than it did to outsiders at the time, but the attempt to break with the past also now seems unproductive and unhelpful. Senior civil servants point to the strength and influence of work on lifelong learning which had been going on under different ministers not only prior to the committee's inquiry, but before devolution. In particular, they had produced *Opportunity Scotland: A paper on lifelong learning* (SOEID 1998). Policy development has continued largely on the basis set out in this document.

Behind the scenes there was tension between the Minister's view of the role of the Enterprise and Lifelong Learning Committee and the role that the committee adopted in relation to this exercise – a pattern which would soon repeat itself with the Education, Culture and Sport Committee. Most of the recommendations of the Enterprise and Lifelong Learning Committee were broadly in line with existing policy, but in one important respect, the committee's report was out of line. This was that young people aged 16 years old and over who had left school were included in the report's recommendations, but because the remit of the committee limited their action in this respect, links to school education were referred to, but not addressed. The idea of a joint enquiry into transitions beyond compulsory education to be undertaken with the Education Committee was suggested, but not taken up.

Instead, in 2002, the Education, Culture and Sport Committee launched its own Inquiry into the Purposes of Scottish Education at the same time as the Minister for Education and Young People initiated a National Debate on Education. The National Debate was reported to have produced a wide-ranging response which went beyond the scope or volume of responses expected for more traditional forms of consultation. This included more than 1500 responses (including over 400 from school pupils) while at least 800 events were organised up and down the country and over 20,000 people were said to have taken a direct part in the exercise. The Inquiry was less successful, receiving between 50 and 60 submissions, commissioning the Scottish Council for Research in Education to run ten focus groups and taking oral evidence on three occasions. In the event the report of the Inquiry (Scottish Parliament 2003) was made in terms similar to the report on the National Debate (SEED/Munn *et al.* 2003), but the policy document which emerged, *Educating for Excellence: Choice and opportunity* (SEED 2003), was clearly a response to the National Debate and made no formal reference to or acknowledgement of the report on the Inquiry.

In effect, both the Inquiry and the National Debate engendered very mixed messages. For example, the report on the Inquiry states that respondents had:

> agreed that Scotland's non-selective system of schooling – usually referred to in the submissions as 'comprehensive education' – has been successful in raising aspirations and levels of achievement

and that

> there is a need for change, *perhaps* of a radical nature, because a rapidly changing world is developing needs which the present system does not meet.
>
> (Scottish Parliament 2003: Para 14/15)

Thus consultation in the new millennium appeared to offer no greater guidance to policy-makers than it did in the last. Any feeling of déjà vu in relation to *Action Plan* may be strengthened when it is added that the key action for the 14–16 age group prompted by the Curriculum Review is that SQA is presently working on new Skills for Work courses and that a working group has been established to examine the issue of FE staff teaching 14–16 year olds.

The high political status of the Curriculum Review is notable in comparison to the earlier policy documents dealt with here. Whereas *Action Plan* appeared to be apolitical and *Higher Still* had only a formal letter of endorsement, the Curriculum Review proposals contain a lengthy introduction jointly signed by the Minister for Education and Young People and his deputy as well as being accompanied by the separate 'Ministerial response'. Thus we see politicians demonstrating that they see the processes of educational policy review and political decision-making as fully linked.

The reason for the two signatures, of course, is also peculiar to the new Scottish political process. Government is by coalition and policy-making comes within the framework of a Partnership

Agreement which sets the Executive to meet 15 'High Level Commitments' and to address 26 action points for 'Supporting Activity'. While the minister is Labour, his deputy is a Liberal Democrat, but they share responsibility for this agenda. Curricular reform comes under a commitment to provide 'more flexible learning and development opportunities so that pupils' experience is matched to their individual needs'. In particular, for 14–18 year olds this means 'assessment methods that support learning and teaching' and for 14–16 year olds 'courses to allow [them] to develop vocational skills . . . and undertake courses in FE colleges as part of a school-based curriculum' (Scottish Executive 2003: 21).

As if to confirm that policy-making is operating in a new context, the Curriculum Review grounds itself in a series of Scottish Executive documents. The Curriculum Review Group's report contains quotations from or references to: the Dewar-Alexander paper, *Social Justice . . . A Scotland where everyone matters* (Scottish Executive 1999); and the National Debate on Education – the most extensive consultation ever of the people of Scotland on the state of school education. However, no mention is made of the parliamentary Inquiry into the Purposes of Scottish Education and indeed the report states clearly that: 'The task of the Review Group was to *identify the purposes of education* 3 to 18 . . .' (SEED 2004a: 7 – emphasis added).

More importantly, perhaps, they refer back to Scottish legislation. The Standards in Scotland's Schools etc. Act 2000 (Scottish Parliament 2000) defined the responsibilities of ministers and increased the accountability of local authorities through the idea of statutory national priorities for education. The national priorities are stated in deliberately broad terms, such as: raising the standards of educational attainment for all in schools; developing the skills of teachers; promoting equality; working with parents to teach pupils respect for themselves and for each other; and equipping pupils with the skills, attitudes and expectations to prosper in a changing society.

The intention here is to create a framework for reporting within which local flexibility and experimentation can be applied. But they are placed in a statutory context which gives politicians, civil servants and local authorities a keen interest in ensuring that they can be reported on and shown to be being acted on.

Policy learning in the Scottish context

In this chapter we have tried to give an account of changes in educational policy-making in Scotland across 30 years, by examining the evidence from three major reforms. In the course of the chapter, we have:

- described the changing political context in which policy-makers have been working as Scotland has taken on devolved powers and begun to develop processes for handling those powers;

- noted that, both before and after devolution, policy-makers have been consistently faced with a dilemma regarding the extent to which they should try to resolve issues in different sectors, or for different age bands, or try to undertake comprehensive or systemic reforms which avoid the negative aspects of piecemeal reform, but also add a level of complexity which brings its own risks;

- noted the extent to which there has been continuity in policy thinking in Scotland over the period, particularly in the path from *Action Plan* to *Higher Still*.

A Curriculum for Excellence shows how education policy is being handled in full post-devolution mode. Here we seem to see new approaches being taken to try to establish policy frameworks which reflect popular opinion, with multiform national consultation being undertaken on principles. Scottish ministers in the Labour–Liberal coalition take a lead role in policy-making, within the framework of an inter-party agreement, and MSPs (Members of the Scottish Parliament) try to influence policy through the work of cross-party committees which have tried to take the initiative in the form of national inquiries. With *A Curriculum for Excellence* we see a return to the approach of the 1970s, with the use of a high-profile committee, rather than a cadre of professionals, to carry out the work. Also we see real attempts being made to decentralise the design and implementation of educational reform, giving local authorities – now more publicly accountable than before – considerable involvement in and responsibility for delivery. It is not clear, however, how far this change arises from lessons learnt, rather than the new political context.

We have examined the form and role of policy learning across a 30-year span of policy-making and have concluded that, while there are clear examples of policy learning (and even more examples of deliberate attempts to secure continuity and continuous improvement on the past), the scope for policy learning may be more restricted than might appear at first sight. In the Scottish context, this has been because of the pace and nature of the reform process, which makes it difficult to establish a basis for real policy learning. But also it is because of rapid changes to the environment within which the reforms have taken place – changes which are likely to invalidate the lessons of earlier policy implementation. We have suggested that a linear model of implementation, review and learning is not always applicable to the realities of reform and, indeed, that in many cases important areas of policy-making may be part of the reform process. In addition, where reforms become increasingly wide ranging and complex, it may be hard to draw lessons from what has gone before. Nonetheless, we have seen that, while policy-making based on systematic and thorough evaluations may be less appropriate than might appear at first sight, there has been a desire among policy-makers to build on what has gone before. All of this suggests that there is a need for the further study both of the nature of policy learning and of the scope for policy learning in the policy-making process in education.

Notes

1. Year classes in Scottish secondary schools are referred to as S1 (secondary 1) or first year to S6 (secondary 6) or sixth year.

2. These SGAs consist of combinations of 160-hour, externally assessed courses, free-standing units and core skills which would normally take one year of full-time study to complete. They are available at six levels and are intended to prepare learners for employment and/or further studies. There are SGAs which specify certain subject requirements and are named accordingly (e.g. SGA in Care or in Sciences) and general SGAs which do not require specific subject content.

References

Scottish Education Department (SED) (1977) *The Structure of the Curriculum in the Third and Fourth Years of the Scottish Secondary School*. Edinburgh: HMSO.

— (1979) *16–18s in Scotland: The first two years of post-compulsory education*. Edinburgh: SED.

— (1983) *16–18s in Scotland: An action plan*. Edinburgh: SED.

Scottish Executive (1999) *Social Justice ... A Scotland where everyone matters*. Edinburgh: Scottish Executive.

— (2003) *A Partnership for A Better Scotland: Partnership Agreement*. Edinburgh: Scottish Executive.

Scottish Executive Education Department (SEED) (2001a) *Circular 3/2001 – Guidance on flexibility in the curriculum*. Edinburgh: Scottish Executive.

— (2001b) *Review of Initial Implementation of New National Qualifications*. A report by the National Qualifications Steering Group to the Scottish Executive. Edinburgh: HMSO.

— (2003) *Educating for Excellence: Choice and opportunity* (The Executive's response to the National Debate). Edinburgh: Scottish Executive.

— (2004a) *A Curriculum for Excellence. Report by the Curriculum Review Group*. Edinburgh: Scottish Executive.

— (2004b) *A Curriculum for Excellence. Ministerial response*. Edinburgh: Scottish Executive.

Scottish Executive Education Department (SEED)/Munn *et al.* (2003) *The National Debate on Education – the Best for All Our Children: Emerging views.* Edinburgh: Scottish Executive.

Scottish Office Education Department (SOED) (1991) *Access and Opportunity.* Edinburgh: HMSO.

– (1992) *Upper Secondary Education in Scotland.* The Howie Report. Edinburgh: HMSO.

– (1994) *Higher Still: Opportunity for all.* Edinburgh: HMSO.

– (1999) *Opportunities and Choices: A consultation paper on post-school provision for 16–18 year olds.* Edinburgh: HMSO.

Scottish Office Education and Industry Department (SOEID) (1998) *Opportunity Scotland: A paper on lifelong learning.* Cm 4048. Edinburgh: HMSO.

Scottish Parliament (2000) Standards in Scotland's Schools etc. Act 2000. Norwich: The Stationery Office.

Scottish Parliament (Education, Culture and Sport Committee) (2003) *Inquiry into the Purposes of Scottish Education. Volume 1: Report.* Norwich: The Stationery Office.

Policy bibliography

Action Plan

HM Government (1986) *Working Together – Education and training.* London: HMSO.

Scottish Education Department (SED) (1977) *16–19 Educational Needs after School.* Report of Conference held on 29 April at Glasgow College of Food Technology. Edinburgh: SED.

— (undated – c.1977) *16–19 Education in Scotland: A discussion document.* Report by HM Inspectors of Schools Committee for Education 16–19. Edinburgh: SED.

— (1979) *16–18s in Scotland: The first two years of post-compulsory education.* Edinburgh: SED.

— (1983) *16–18s in Scotland: An action plan.* Edinburgh: SED.

Higher Still

Higher Still Development Unit (1995) *Principles for the Post-16 Curriculum – Consultation document.* Edinburgh: Scottish Consultative Committee on the Curriculum.

Scottish Executive Education Department (SEED) (2001) *Review of Initial Implementation of New National Qualifications.* A report by the National Qualifications Steering Group to the Scottish Executive. Edinburgh: HMSO.

Scottish Office Education Department (SOED) (1991) *Access and Opportunity.* Edinburgh: HMSO.

— (1992) *Upper Secondary Education in Scotland.* The Howie Report. Edinburgh: HMSO.

— (1994) *Higher Still: Opportunity for all.* Edinburgh: HMSO.

A Curriculum for Excellence

Scottish Executive (1999) *Social Justice . . . A Scotland where everyone matters.* Edinburgh: Scottish Executive.

— (2003) *A Partnership for a Better Scotland: Partnership Agreement.* Edinburgh: Scottish Executive.

Scottish Executive Education Department (SEED) (2000) *Improving our Schools: A consultation paper on national priorities for schools education in Scotland.* Edinburgh: Scottish Executive.

— (2001) *Guidance on Flexibility in the Curriculum.* Circular 3/2001. Edinburgh: Scottish Executive.

— (2003) *Educating for Excellence: Choice and opportunity* (The Executive's response to the National Debate). Edinburgh: Scottish Executive.

— (2004a) *A Curriculum for Excellence: Report by the Curriculum Review Group.* Edinburgh: Scottish Executive.

— (2004b) *A Curriculum for Excellence: Ministerial response.* Edinburgh: Scottish Executive.

— (2004) *Ambitious, Excellent Schools: Our agenda for action.* Edinburgh: Scottish Executive.

— (2004) *Building the Foundations of a Lifelong Learning Society: A review of collaboration between schools and further education colleges in Scotland.* Interim Report. Edinburgh: Scottish Executive.

— (2005) *Guidance on the Appropriate Age and Stage when Young People can be Presented for Externally Assessed Qualifications.* Circular 03/July05. Edinburgh: Scottish Executive.

Scottish Executive Education Department (SEED)/Munn *et al.* (2003) *The National Debate on Education – the Best for All Our Children: Emerging views.* Edinburgh: Scottish Executive.

Scottish Office Education Department (SOED) (1999) *Opportunities and Choices: A consultation paper on post-school provision for 16–18 year olds.* Edinburgh: HMSO.

Scottish Parliament (2000) Standards in Scotland's Schools etc. Act 2000. Norwich: The Stationery Office.

Scottish Parliament (Education, Culture and Sport Committee) (2003) *Inquiry into the Purposes of Scottish Education. Volume 1: Report.* Norwich: The Stationery Office.

Scottish Parliament (Enterprise and Lifelong Learning Committee) (2002) *Final Report on Lifelong Learning.* Norwich: The Stationery Office.

6 Learning from 'home international' comparisons: 14–19 policy across the United Kingdom

David Raffe

Introduction

In this chapter I argue that policy differences among the home countries of the United Kingdom provide opportunities for policy learning. These opportunities are increasing as a result of policy divergence since the Scottish Parliament and the Welsh and Northern Irish Assemblies were established in 1999. However, 'home international' comparisons provided opportunities for policy learning long before 1999. This potential is still under-exploited, partly because of a tendency for policy-makers to confuse policy learning with policy borrowing.

Difference and divergence in 14–19 policy

The governments of England, Wales, Scotland and Northern Ireland face similar policy issues in 14–19 education and training and many of their policy objectives are similar. They all aim to increase attainment, to raise participation and to reduce barriers to progression at 16. They all aim to stretch the most able and to combat disaffection and disengagement. They all aim to develop a more coherent framework of opportunities that cater for young people of all abilities, backgrounds and interests, provide more choice and facilitate flexible progression. They all aim to enhance vocational provision, as a means of motivating learners and of meeting future skill needs. They all aim to help young people to acquire core and transferable skills and to promote responsible citizenship and healthy lifestyles.

In pursuing such objectives, a government must make a number of strategic choices. It must decide on the structure of pathways, and choose between a 'track-based' approach, which preserves separate vocational and academic tracks and encourages each to develop a distinctive identity, and a 'unified' approach, which brings all pathways into a single framework; or it may settle for an intermediate 'linkages' approach which retains separate tracks but increases the links between them. It must decide how to structure progression: whether, for example, to treat the end of compulsory education as a natural break, or to develop the concept of a single stage (such as 14–19) which straddles compulsory and post-compulsory learning and the dispersal of young people to different institutions and modes of learning. It must also choose between alternative curricular models, for example, a baccalaureate model with common requirements for all learners, or a 'climbing-frame' model which allows more curricular choice and flexible progression with multiple entry and exit points. It must decide how to organise work-based provision, and how far to integrate it or keep it separate from institution-based learning. And it must make numerous more detailed decisions, such as how to provide for more generic learning outcomes like core skills and citizenship, how to promote institutional collaboration, and how to encourage pedagogical and curricular innovation.

Despite their similar policy objectives, the administrations in England, Wales and Scotland have made different responses to these strategic choices.

At the beginning of 2003, the government in England seemed to have decided on a unified approach after two decades of fluctuating between track-based and linkages approaches. It appointed the Tomlinson Working Group to develop proposals for a unified framework of 14–19 qualifications. The Working Group proposed a system of diplomas at four levels, with a common core, and with flexible opportunities and incentives for progression (Working Group on 14–19 Reform 2004). The Working Group's vision was a unified framework based on a compromise between baccalaureate and climbing-frame features.

However, the Government rejected this vision in its White Paper of February 2005 (DfES 2005a); England is once again committed to a track-based approach with linkages between the tracks. GCSEs and A levels remain the 'cornerstones' of the system. The specialised diplomas, which Tomlinson had proposed as part of a flexible and unified structure are, instead, being developed as a separate vocational track potentially starting at 14 years. The Government remains committed to the principle of 14–19 as a stage, an idea which had been promoted by the Technical and Vocational Education Initiative (TVEI) of the 1980s and which became part of New Labour thinking in the 1990s (Chitty 2004). The Government accepted Tomlinson's proposal to include work-based and institution-based provision, as far as possible, within a common framework. However, they will serve different functions: work-based apprenticeships will prepare for direct entry to employment while institution-based specialised diplomas will provide a broad-based foundation for further education and training (DfES 2005b). The Government had earlier decided to base all work-based provision, except at the very lowest level, on apprenticeship, while retaining its role as a safety-net for young people who cannot find jobs or learning opportunities elsewhere.

Wales, like England, is committed to the concept of a 14–19 stage as a basis for planning and organising provision. This commitment is expressed principally through the *14–19 Learning Pathways*, a flagship policy of the Welsh Assembly Government (2004). The Learning Pathways are driven by the principles of entitlement, inclusion, the community school and new learning pedagogies (Egan

2004). They are based on six elements: individually tailored learning pathways, wider choice and flexibility, a learning core, a learning coach, individual support, and careers advice and guidance. The pathways retain distinct academic and vocational programmes but they transform their relationship and potentially their content by placing them within a unified framework. The Learning Pathways exemplify the 'linkages' approach described above, but compared with current English policies they are closer to the unified end of the continuum from track-based to unified approaches. They are likely to be increasingly based on a baccalaureate model, in the form of the Welsh Baccalaureate, currently being piloted. This is an overarching certificate, based on existing academic and vocational qualifications together with a common core, which will be available at Foundation, Intermediate and Advanced levels. The Learning Pathways embrace work-based provision as well as institution-based provision. In contrast to England, where apprenticeships and specialised diplomas will have distinct roles, it is proposed to develop 'combined apprenticeships' to bridge work-based and full-time pathways (Chapman 2005).

The Scottish Executive has not adopted 14–19 as a stage for planning or organising education. There are separate governance and funding arrangements for school and post-school learning, while curriculum and qualifications have hitherto been organised around 5–14, 14–16 and post-16 stages. From 1999 the *Higher Still* reform introduced a 'unified curriculum and assessment system' of new National Qualifications (NQs), which aimed to embrace all academic and vocational institution-based learning beyond 16, below the level of higher education. Higher Still's unified approach was chosen after an alternative track-based approach was decisively rejected in a public consultation (Scottish Office 1994). However, work-based provision, which (as in Wales) is organised around apprenticeship and non-apprenticeship modes, is (unlike Wales) not included within the unified framework.

Higher Still's curricular model, designed especially to promote access and progression, is a climbing-frame model of units and courses at seven levels. Schools have found the new NQs useful in 14–16 provision as well as post-16, partly because of their promise of better progression (Howieson *et al.* 2004). The relation between Standard Grades (14–16 courses) and the new NQs is under review. Scotland is unlikely to adopt 14–19 as an organising stage of education but it is moving towards a progression-oriented framework for curriculum and qualifications that straddles the current thresholds at 14 years as well as 16. This framework is being developed as part of *A Curriculum for Excellence*, the review of the 3–18 school curriculum which aims to develop 'successful learners, confident individuals, responsible citizens and effective contributors to society and at work' (SEED 2004a: 12; SEED 2004b).

In Northern Ireland, as in Scotland, education and training tend to be organised around sectors rather than stages. For a long time, the debate over the future of selection at 11 distracted policy attention from 14–19 issues. The Direct Rule Government aims to resolve this debate by abolishing academic selection at 11, maintaining a diversity of secondary institutions and introducing a curriculum Entitlement Framework which will guarantee a range of academic and vocational options for learners at 14-plus and at 16-plus (Smith 2005). Different types of schools and colleges will work collaboratively to offer curriculum options. The age of 14 appears to be emerging as an important decision point in the Northern Ireland education system and the notion of a 14–19 stage has entered the discourse of the government as a basis for reviewing and planning provision (Hain 2005). It remains to be seen how the options guaranteed by the Entitlement Framework will be presented to learners and which curriculum patterns or pathways will emerge from their choices. Modern Apprenticeships will continue to be organised separately.

The home countries are thus pursuing different policy solutions to similar problems. These differences are not all the result of the 1999 devolution settlement. The administratively devolved arrangements before 1999 permitted a substantial degree of autonomy to Scotland and Northern Ireland and, more recently, to Wales. Nevertheless, the democratic devolution of 1999 increased the devolved administrations' powers and made it easier for them to resist the imposition of 'English' policies and to pursue domestic initiatives, such as the Welsh Baccalaureate, which had not been politically possible previously. Especially in Wales, it allowed domestic policy-making to proceed more strategically than was previously possible, with less uncertainty surrounding the political limits to autonomy. As a result, the home countries' 14–19 policies are not only different, they are currently diverging, although it is still too soon to judge the extent of divergence or say how long the process will be sustained (Raffe 2005).

Learning from home international comparisons

These policy differences make comparisons among the home countries of the UK – or what I shall call 'home international' comparisons – a promising source of policy learning. By home international comparisons, I refer in particular to the kinds of systematic comparisons conducted by academic researchers, but the argument also applies to the more informal comparative knowledge of policy-makers and practitioners, and to the use of international comparisons and examples in policy-making and in wider policy debates.

It is often hard to draw practical conclusions when we compare policies with overseas countries because of differences in the education systems and in their social, economic and cultural contexts. The 'other things' are not 'equal'. However, these differences are smaller among the home countries. While there are institutional differences there are also common features, including the basic institutional framework of schools, colleges and training providers, the concepts and structures which organise the curriculum, and the character and functions of qualifications. Moreover, the social, economic and cultural contexts of education in the home countries are similar, at least compared with other countries. England, Wales, Scotland and (to a somewhat lesser extent) Northern Ireland share a common, integrated labour market, and they have similar social systems, family structures and youth cultures, as reflected for example in a 'British' pattern of early transitions to adulthood (Cavalli and Galland 1995). Therefore, when we compare policy innovations across the home countries of the UK, it is more likely that any differences in their achievement of policy objectives, in the unintended consequences of policies or in the practical issues involved in developing and implementing them reflect differences in the policies rather than in their contexts.

Rose (1993) lists seven factors which influence the transferability of programmes or policies from one time or place to another. These are the 'uniqueness' of the programme, the substitutability of the institutions which deliver it, the equivalence of resources, the complexity of cause-and-effect models underlying the programme, the scale of the change, the interdependence of the jurisdictions concerned and the congruity of their values. Many of the conditions for successful policy transfer – such as substitutable institutions, equivalent resources, interdependent jurisdictions and congruous values – are more likely to apply when policies are transferred from one home country to another than when policies are imported from more distant countries. Policy borrowing – the identification and appropriation of 'best practice' from other countries – is a notoriously unreliable method of policy development; nevertheless, policy borrowing between the home countries of the UK is more likely to be successful than policy borrowing from other countries.

However, the more important contribution of home international comparisons is to support a concept of *policy learning* that is very much broader than mere *policy borrowing*. Just as it may be relatively easy to transfer programmes or policies between the home countries of the UK, so can an understanding of how policies work and of the practical issues in developing and implementing them, be more easily transferred. And because of this greater transferability, it may be easier to draw lessons from policy differences, when they occur.

Purposes of policy learning

Commentators have identified a wide range of purposes of cross-national comparative research in education (Phillips 1999; Green 2002). Those relevant to policy development include:

- helping us to understand our own system better, by comparing it with other types of system and by providing benchmarks for its performance

- identifying cross-national trends and pressures which affect education and training in all countries

- identifying policy options and clarifying alternative strategies

- comparing the impact of different policy options

- helping us to understand educational processes and policy issues by observing a wider range of policy approaches and/or of contexts in which they are applied

- helping us to understand the processes of educational change

- clarifying the scope for, and limitations of, national autonomy in education policy

- supporting the cross-national co-ordination of policies, institutions and practices

- providing practical information for learners, providers and other stakeholders whose interests cross national borders.

Home international comparisons can support all of these kinds of policy learning.

Helping us to understand our own system better

Cross-national comparisons can make us aware of features of our own education system that we take for granted, or features that it lacks but which are present elsewhere. Comparisons with systems that are very different are more likely to generate radical insights of this kind, but home international comparisons may pinpoint more specific features. They can alert us to potential strengths on which current reforms should build, such as the tradition of local innovation in England or the clear and distinctive missions of schools and colleges in Scotland. They can also alert us to weaknesses; for example, Anglo-Scottish comparisons draw attention to the barriers to progression within English 14–19 education and to the structural separation of school- and work-based provision in Scotland. Educational performance is often benchmarked against other home countries, partly to ensure competitiveness within UK higher education and labour markets, but also because these countries provide an indication of what is achievable in the UK context. For example, the experience of Scotland and Northern Ireland suggests that a 50 per cent participation rate in higher education for England is achievable, although it also suggests that it might have been better to pursue other priorities.

Identifying cross-national trends or pressures

International comparisons can prevent countries from engaging in a fruitless search for country-specific solutions to problems that are cross-national. For example, numerous attempts have been made to promote 'parity of esteem' for vocational and general education in England. These reflect a widespread belief that vocational education has lower status in England than elsewhere, which is often attributed to the way that education developed along social class lines. But in Scotland, whose education system developed along more inclusive and national lines, vocational education has *lower* status at 16-plus than in England (Raffe *et al.* 2001a). Inequality of esteem and pressures for academic drift are cross-national phenomena (Lasonen 1996; Green *et al.* 1999). Comparisons with other countries help to challenge the assumption of 'English exceptionalism' – the belief, widespread among researchers and commentators, that education and training in England are not only distinctive but distinctively pathological (Raffe 2002). Home international comparisons also serve the more specific purpose of identifying trends or pressures that are common to the countries of the UK, even if they are not necessarily found elsewhere. For example, the problem of low participation in post-compulsory education is UK-wide. Contrary to common belief, Scotland's more flexible course structure has not encouraged consistently higher participation (Raffe *et al.* 2001b). The UK's low participation rate is not primarily a product of educational arrangements, which vary across the home countries. It is mainly caused by contextual factors which are UK-wide, such as the labour market and, possibly, cultural patterns of transition to adulthood. A policy for raising participation that ignores these wider determinants is unlikely to be effective.

Identifying policy options and clarifying alternative strategies

In much the same way that cross-national comparisons can make us aware of taken-for-granted features of our education system, or of features that are absent, such comparisons can also give us new insights into current policies and into possible alternatives. Our understanding of the alternative policy strategies listed at the beginning of this chapter (track-based versus unified, baccalaureate versus climbing frame, and so on) has been shaped and refined by home international comparisons. In the 1990s, policy analysts drew on comparisons between Scotland and England to develop models of track-based and unified systems of post-16 provision; developments in Wales influenced further distinctions between baccalaureate and framework models of a unified approach (IPPR 1990; NCE 1993; Hodgson and Spours 2003). The Tomlinson Working Group drew on home international differences when it distinguished between climbing-frame and baccalaureate models, and proposed a framework with features of both (Working Group on 14–19 Reform 2003).

Comparing the impact of different policy options

The devolved administrations have been described as 'natural laboratories' for policy experimentation, although at times they have rather provided the control groups against which to compare experimental reforms in England (Adams and Schmuecker 2005). The policy divergence summarised at the beginning of this chapter, together with the relatively small institutional and contextual differences among the home countries, suggest that home international comparisons may provide opportunities for quasi-experimental, 'what works' studies of 14–19 policy. For example, Croxford (2001) found higher levels of social segregation, wider variation in school value-added and wider social inequalities in attainment in England, where school policies emphasised choice and diversity, than in the more uniform comprehensive systems of Scotland and Wales. However, this comparison was based on a single cohort and could not confidently attribute the differences in outcomes to differences in policy. A more recent study found that class inequalities declined in Scotland relative to England in the 1980s and 1990s; this divergent trend might be linked to divergent policies for school choice and markets, although the study concluded that any link was likely to be indirect (Croxford and Raffe

2006). As this example illustrates, it can be difficult to draw firm conclusions about 'what works' from correlating policy differences with differences in outcomes in a sample of only four home countries. However, even negative conclusions may be important in policy terms. For example, policy-makers attributing England's relatively favourable Programme for International Student Assessment (PISA) results to school reforms must explain how Scotland and Northern Ireland achieved similar results without such reforms.

Helping us to understand educational processes and policy issues

Home international comparisons may be particularly useful as a source of practical knowledge for policy development, including knowledge about the educational processes that policies aim to influence, or about the practical issues that arise in implementation. This type of knowledge depends on a broad range of experience from which reformers can learn. Governments often introduce pilot or exploratory measures based on diversity and local innovation, such as the 14–19 Pathfinders in England, in order that later generations of the reform can learn from the different approaches they have explored. By the same logic, home international comparisons can broaden the range of experience from which to learn. For example, by pooling the home countries' experience of core or key skills we can find a wider range of models of delivery (discrete, integrated, embedded, signposted), certification arrangements and incentives to learners and providers (Hodgson et al. 2004). We can similarly observe a wider range of approaches to school self-management by conducting comparisons across home countries as well as within them (Raab et al. 1997). Studying historical as well as current experience further extends the diversity of experience from which to learn. For example, the QCA's Framework for Achievement in England may learn as much from the

Scottish experience of unitisation in the 1980s as from the Welsh and Scottish credit frameworks today.

Helping us to understand the processes of educational change

The home countries are diverging with respect to the process of educational change as well as the content and direction of such change (Raffe 2005). This is a further source of policy learning. The Nuffield Review of 14–19 Education is currently paying particular attention to Wales as a source of policy learning about process-led models of curricular change and about the consultative process of developing the *14–19 Learning Pathways* (Hayward et al. 2005). An earlier comparison of *Curriculum 2000* in England and *Higher Still* in Scotland drew lessons for reforms of curriculum and qualifications. These included: the need for time for consultation and development; the need to agree long-term goals even if the process of achieving them is incremental; the need to anticipate conflicts inherent in the design of any unified system; the lessons from the fact that both reforms led to exams crises; and so on (Hodgson et al. 2004).

Clarifying the scope for, and limitations of, national autonomy in education policy

Comparative research has tended to move away from studies of national education systems as separate, self-contained units of comparison in favour of studies of the relationships between systems (Green 2002). This perspective is particularly applicable to the study of the four interrelated systems of the UK. The autonomy of the devolved administrations is determined not only by the constitutional arrangements of 1999, but also by the functional interdependence of the four systems. For example, Wales' freedom to reform qualifications is restricted by the desire to protect the competitive position of Welsh young people in the higher education and labour markets of the UK. Hence the choice of an overarching certificate, the Welsh Baccalaureate Qualification, which retains within it qualifications that are recognised across the UK. The imposition of top-up fees for higher education in England has further exposed the dependent position of the devolved administrations. Such aspects of interdependence are a relatively unexplored area of home international research.

Supporting the cross-national co-ordination of policies, institutions and practices

Home international comparisons can help the respective governments to co-ordinate their policies by clarifying the interdependent features of the four systems, as mentioned above, and by analysing the different institutional settings in which co-ordinated policies are placed. For example, the UK-wide Sector Skills Councils (SSCs) require a sophisticated understanding of the different institutional structures with which they interact. Similarly, an understanding of institutional differences is required to co-ordinate the home countries' credit and qualification frameworks.

Providing practical information for other stakeholders whose interests cross national borders

Learners, providers, employers and other stakeholders have a similar need for information on home international differences that goes beyond the purely descriptive.

These examples show that home international comparisons have the potential to support a concept of policy learning that is much broader than policy borrowing. How far is this potential realised in practice?

'Home international' policy learning in practice

Bowe *et al.* (1992) distinguish three contexts of policy-making, which they term the context of influence, the context of policy text production, and the context of practice. Home international comparisons have played a larger role in the context of influence, and possibly in the context of practice, than in the context of policy text production. With respect to the context of influence, they have played a role in the debates about the post-16 (and more recently 14–19) curriculum and qualifications. From the Institute for Public Policy Research's (IPPR's) (1990) 'British *Baccalauréat*' to the current 14–19 Alliance, English advocates of more unified frameworks have been influenced by the experience of Scotland and, more recently, of Wales. In Scotland, Anglo-Scottish comparisons have been used to argue that Scotland should retain its more flexible course structure in order to sustain higher participation levels (McPherson 1992). Independent policy bodies such as the National Commission on Education in the 1990s and the Nuffield Review of 14–19 Education in the present decade, have championed home international comparisons and made substantial use of them, alongside comparisons with other countries (NCE 1993; Hayward *et al.* 2005).

In the context of policy text production, however, there appears to be much less mutual learning among the home countries. Before political devolution, in 1996–97, I interviewed policy-makers in the four home countries of the UK about their use of home international comparisons to inform policy decision-making in 14–19 education and training (Raffe 1998). They all recognised the considerable potential for such comparisons to inform policy. But they also agreed that home international comparisons – or at least, the more systematic comparisons of the kind carried out by academic researchers – had very little influence on policy-making in practice. More recent interviews conducted in 2004, several years after political devolution, suggested that this was still the case (Byrne and Raffe 2005). Trench's (2005) review of inter-governmental relations since devolution does not mention mutual policy learning as either a purpose or an outcome of these relations.

Mutual learning may take place in the third context described by Bowe *et al.* (1992), that of practice, but this typically happens informally, through institutional links and movements of staff and students between the home countries.

There are several reasons why home international comparisons have little influence on policy-making, at least within the context of policy text production.

First, there are the usual difficulties of linking policy and research: different timescales, different purposes and frames of reference, poor communications and inadequate mutual understanding, and the paucity of data and of available research to inform immediate research agendas (Nutley 2003). However, the types of home international comparisons with which this chapter is concerned are broader than academic research.

A second reason concerns the nature of mutual exchanges among the UK administrations. These exchanges focus on policy co-ordination, on smoothing over differences among the home countries rather than learning from them. Such exchanges may be informed by comparative information about home international differences, but they provide little scope or encouragement for broader policy learning. They are forward-looking, concerned more with developing policies for the future than with examining the effects of past policies. Consequently, when policy-makers are influenced by policies elsewhere it is often the policy idea that inspires them, rather than the experience of the policy in practice. Several recent examples of policy borrowing between the home countries are of this kind. For example, the English Learning and Skills Councils and the Scottish all-age guidance agency Careers Scotland were both influenced by similar reform proposals in Wales, but in both cases the Welsh reforms were still in development and there was no empirical experience from which to learn.

A third reason is the tendency for policy-makers to understand policy learning from other countries as policy borrowing – identifying and copying best practice – rather than the broader notion of policy learning advocated in this chapter. As a result, policy-makers fail to engage in many forms of policy learning because they do not recognise their potential benefits. Moreover, they tend to narrow their choice of comparator countries to those that are perceived to exemplify best practice. If best practice is inferred from a country's success in educational or economic terms, the home countries may appear too alike in their educational and economic performance to choose each other as comparators. For this reason, many Scottish policy-makers have followed the example of the 1992 Howie Report (SEED 1992) that looked for comparators in continental Europe rather than elsewhere in the UK. Alternatively, if best practice is identified on political grounds, and comparator countries chosen for their political or ideological stance, England may be reluctant to learn from Wales or Scotland, and vice versa, as these countries represent conflicting strands of New Labour thinking (Paterson 2003). For the same reason, Wales and Scotland are more disposed to learn from each other. David Miliband, appointed English Minister of State for School Standards in 2002, provided a rare exception when he paid his first ministerial study visit to Scotland rather than the more exotic locations offered by his officials.

Finally, the unequal relationships among the four administrations, and the complex 'politics of similarity and difference' within each home country, inhibit objective comparison and policy learning. Before political devolution, the asymmetrical pattern of decision-making and the unequal power relations between administrations made it difficult for policy-makers to treat intra-UK policy differences as subjects of objective comparison. Policy-makers in Scotland, Wales and Northern Ireland were preoccupied with a complicated game in which they protected their autonomy by variously anticipating, resisting, deferring, adapting or 'badging' policy initiatives from England (Raffe 1998). Such relationships provided little scope for policy learning other than of a defensive kind. Since 1999, the devolution settlement has provided more of the openness and political space necessary for policy learning. Nevertheless, educational policy is still bound up with issues of national identity and a desire to emphasise policy differences. This is especially the case in Wales, which has asserted the 'clear red water' between its own policies and those of England more strongly than Scotland (Egan and James 2003). Like Scotland, Wales has looked towards Europe for policy learning and has played a leading role in the European Association of Regional and Local Authorities for Lifelong Learning.

Conclusion

How can the potential for policy learning from home international comparisons be more fully realised? Four things might help.

The first is simply more encouragement and support for home international research, especially by academic researchers. Academic research tends to be organised and often funded at a UK level, and comparative research within the UK may present fewer practical difficulties than research involving countries elsewhere. Programmes such as the Economic and Social Research Council (ESRC) Teaching and Learning Research Programme encourage researchers to exploit the research potential of differences in policy and practice across the UK. Other organisations which fund or broker policy research, such as the Learning and Skills Development Agency, have also shown an interest in home international comparisons (Byrne and Raffe 2005).

Academic educational researchers are relatively likely to see comparative research as broader than a source of policy borrowing. They have defended, often amidst controversy, a view of research that emphasises its critical and interpretative roles, as well as the identification of 'what works'. Moreover, the current climate within the devolved administrations, and to an extent within the London government, recognises the role of academic research alongside other sources of systematic evidence to support policy-making.

Second, the education policy community needs to acquire a broader concept of policy learning. Many policy-makers currently perceive cross-national comparisons primarily as a source of policy borrowing. In doing so, they are criticised for identifying best practice on the basis of superficial analyses, for failing to allow for differences of context, for seeking a quick fix rather than trying to understand the reasons why policies do (or do not) work, and for borrowing policies on the basis of their political or ideological provenance rather than their effectiveness or transferability (Finegold *et al.* 1992, 1993; Le Métais 2000; Ochs and Phillips 2002). Even within the UK policies can rarely be copied directly from one home country to another. They need to be studied in context and it is the lessons from their experience rather than the policies themselves which are transferable. These lessons often consist of a deeper understanding of the reasons for the success of policies in their home country, of their possible unintended consequences and of the practical issues involved in developing and implementing them, rather than a simple repertoire of best practice. Policy learning is much broader than policy borrowing.

The third factor is a more collaborative model of governance, which emphasises networks and participation rather than hierarchy and command-and-control relationships between government and governed (see Chapter 1). A collaborative model allows more interchange between Bowe *et al.*'s (1992) context of policy text production – where relatively little home international learning takes place – and the contexts of influence and of practice where it occurs more frequently, if often informally. A collaborative model involves the multifaceted relationships between policy-makers and researchers that are required to generate and communicate diverse and complex types of policy knowledge. In a collaborative model, policy learning is sustained through political contestation rather than marginalised or distorted by it.

The final factor is an increased readiness by policy-makers in the four home countries to learn from each other. This assumes a rejection of the politics of similarity and difference described above. Devolution may be stimulating greater political maturity and openness to learning from elsewhere. With their democratic mandates the devolved administrations have less need to play identity politics or engage in policy badging in order to establish their legitimacy. We are becoming readier to admit that we can learn from each other.

Acknowledgements

This chapter is a product of the research project on *Education and Youth Transitions in England, Scotland and Wales, 1984–2002*, supported by the UK Economic and Social Research Council (R000239852). Parts of the text draw on CES Briefing No. 34, *Policy Learning from Home International Comparisons*, written with Delma Byrne. An earlier version was presented to a workshop at the Nuffield Foundation, London and some of the ideas have been tested in seminars or presentations at Dysg (Cardiff), the Scottish Further Education Unit (Stirling) and the University of Exeter. Responsibility for errors and interpretations is, of course, my own.

References

Adams, J. and Schmuecker, K. (eds) (2005) *Devolution in Practice 2006: Public policy differences within the UK*. London: Institute of Public Policy Research (IPPR).

Bowe, R. and Ball, S. with Gold, A. (1992) *Reforming Education and Changing Schools: Case studies in policy sociology*. London: Routledge.

Byrne, D. and Raffe, D. (2005) *Establishing a UK 'Home International' Comparative Research Programme for Post-compulsory Learning*. Learning and Skills Research Centre (LSRC) Research Report. London: Learning and Skills Development Agency (LSDA).

Cavalli, A. and Galland, O. (eds) (1995) *Youth in Europe*. London: Pinter.

Chapman, C. (2005) *14–19 Learning Pathways in Wales*. Cardiff: Welsh Assembly Government, Cardiff.

Chitty, C. (2004) *Education Policy in Britain*. Basingstoke: Palgrave.

Croxford, L. (2001) 'School differences and school education: comparisons between England, Wales and Scotland'. *Education Review*, 15 (1), 68–73.

Croxford, L. and Raffe, D. (2006) 'Education markets and social class inequality: a comparison of trends in England, Scotland and Wales'. Edinburgh: Centre for Educational Sociology, University of Edinburgh.

Department for Education and Skills (DfES) (2005a) *14–19 Education and Skills*. Cm 6476. Norwich: The Stationery Office.

— (2005b) *14–19 Education and Skills: Implementation plan*. Annesley: DfES.

Egan, D. (2004) '14–19 developments in Wales: learning pathways'. Working Paper 19, Nuffield Review of 14–19 Education and Training. Online. Available HTTP: http://www.nuffield14–19review.org.uk (accessed 11 January 2006).

Egan, D. and James, R. (2003) 'Education'. In J. Osmond and J. Jones (eds), *Birth of Welsh Democracy: The first term of the National Assembly for Wales*. Cardiff: Institute of Welsh Affairs.

Finegold, D., McFarland, L. and Richardson, W. (eds) (1992, 1993) 'Something borrowed, something blue? A study of the Thatcher government's appropriation of American education policy', Edited special issue containing Parts 1 and 2. *Oxford Studies in Comparative Education*, Part 1, 2 (2), 1–60; and Part 2, 3 (1), 1–128.

Green, A. (2002) 'Education, globalisation and the role of comparative research'. Professorial Lecture. London: Institute of Education, University of London.

Green, A., Wolf, A. and Leney, T. (1999) *Convergence and Divergence in European*

Education and Training Systems. Bedford Way Papers. London: Institute of Education, University of London.

Hain, P. (2005) Speech by Secretary of State on Outcome of Review of Public Administration: 22 November. Online. Available HTTP: http://www.nio.gov.uk/media-detail.htm?newsID=12513 (accessed 25 January 2006).

Hayward, G., Hodgson, A., Johnson, J., Oancea, A., Pring, R., Spours, K., Wilde, S. and Wright, S. (2005) *Nuffield Review of 14–19 Education and Training: Annual Report 2004–05*. Oxford: University of Oxford Department of Educational Studies.

Hodgson, A. and Spours, K. (2003) *Beyond A levels*. London: Kogan Page.

Hodgson, A., Howieson, C., Raffe, D., Spours, K. and Tinklin, T. (2004) 'Post-16 curriculum and qualifications reforms in England and Scotland: lessons from home international comparisons'. *Journal of Education and Work*, 17 (4), 441–65.

Howieson, C., Raffe, D. and Tinklin, T. (2004) 'The use of new National Qualifications in S3 and S4 in 2002–03'. *Scottish Educational Review*, 36 (2), 177–90.

Institute for Public Policy Research (IPPR) (1990) *A British 'Baccalauréat'?* London: IPPR.

Lasonen, J. (ed.) (1996) *Reforming Upper Secondary Education in Europe*. Jyväskylä: Institute for Educational Research, University of Jyväskylä.

Le Métais, J. (2000) 'Snakes and ladders: learning from international comparisons'. In R. Alexander, M. Osborn and D. Phillips (eds), *Learning from Comparing: New directions in comparative educational research. Volume 2*. Wallingford: Symposium.

McPherson, A. (1992) 'The Howie Report on post-compulsory schooling'. In L. Paterson and D. McCrone (eds), *Scottish Government Yearbook 1992*. Edinburgh: Unit for the Study of Government in Scotland.

National Commission on Education (NCE) (1993) *Learning to Succeed*. London: Heinemann.

Nutley, S. (2003) 'Bridging the policy/research divide: reflections and lessons from the UK'. St Andrews: Research Unit for Research Utilisation, University of St Andrews.

Ochs, K. and Phillips, D. (2002) 'Comparative studies and "cross-national attraction" in education: a typology for the analysis of English interest in educational policy and provision in Germany'. *Oxford Review of Education*, 28 (4), 325–29.

Paterson, L. (2003) 'The three educational ideologies of the British Labour Party, 1997–2001'. *Oxford Review of Education*, 29 (2), 165–86.

Phillips, D. (1999) 'On comparing'. In R. Alexander, P. Broadfoot and D. Phillips (eds), *Learning From Comparing: New directions in comparative educational research. Volume 1*. Wallingford: Symposium.

Raab, C., Munn, P., McAvoy, L., Bailey, L., Arnott, M. and Adler, M. (1997) 'Devolving the management of schools in Britain'. *Educational Administration Quarterly*, 33 (2), 140–57.

Raffe, D. (1998) 'Does learning begin at home? The place of "home international" comparisons in UK policy-making'. *Journal of Education Policy*, 13, 591–602.

— (2002) 'The issues, some reflections, and possible next steps'. In Nuffield Foundation (ed.) *14–19 Education: Papers arising from a seminar series held at the Nuffield Foundation, December 2001–January 2002*. London: Nuffield Foundation.

— (2005) 'Devolution and divergence in education policy'. In J. Adams and K. Schmuecker (eds) *Devolution in Practice 2006: Public policy differences within the UK*. London: Institute for Public Policy Research (IPPR).

Raffe, D., Brannen, K., Fairgrieve, J. and Martin, C. (2001a) 'Participation, inclusiveness, academic drift and parity of esteem: a comparison of post-compulsory education and training in England, Wales, Scotland and Northern Ireland'. *Oxford Review of Education*, 27 (2), 173–203.

Raffe, D., Croxford, L. and Brannen, K. (2001b) 'Participation in full-time education beyond 16: a home international comparison'. *Research Papers in Education*, 16 (1), 43–68.

Rose, R. (1993) *Lesson-drawing in Public Policy: A guide to learning across time and space*. Chatham, NJ: Chatham House.

Scottish Executive Education Department (SEED) (1992) *Upper Secondary Education in Scotland*. The Howie Report. Edinburgh: HMSO.

— (2004a) *A Curriculum for Excellence. A Report by the Curriculum Review Group*. Edinburgh: Scottish Executive.

— (2004b) *A Curriculum for Excellence. Ministerial response*. Edinburgh: Scottish Executive.

Scottish Office (1994) *Higher Still: Opportunity for all*. Edinburgh: HMSO.

Smith, A. (2005) *New Post-Primary Arrangements: A statement by Angela Smith, MP, Minister for Education*. Belfast: Department of Education.

Trench, A. (2005) 'Intergovernmental relations within the UK: the pressures yet to come'. In A. Trench (ed.) *The Dynamics of Devolution: The state of the nations 2005*. Exeter: Imprint Academic.

Welsh Assembly Government (2004) *Learning Pathways 14–19 Guidance*. Circular 37/2004. Cardiff: Department for Training and Education.

Working Group on 14–19 Reform (2003) *Principles for Reform of 14–19 Learning Programmes and Qualifications*. Annesley: DfES Publications.

— (2004) *14–19 Curriculum and Qualifications Reform: Final report*. Annesley: DfES Publications.

7 A framework for understanding and comparing 14–19 education policies in the United Kingdom

Cathleen Stasz and Susannah Wright

Introduction

Forming a picture of policy for 14–19 education in the United Kingdom is a bit like the proverbial blind man confronted by an elephant. It is possible to understand specific parts, but the size, shape and sheer complexity of the elephant remain obscure. With devolution, it has been argued that the four home countries may become increasingly diverse (Raffe 2000). So even as the blind man explores, the elephant may be transforming into an altogether different creature.

Many observers have noted that UK policy seems to proceed without memory and without strategy. Despite the emphasis on 'evidence-based policy' there is little sign that 14–19 education policy makes use of evidence, whether it results from analysis or practical experience.

While a number of recent studies have analysed policies related to 14–19 education, they have some limitations for comparative purposes. Many analyses focus on particular programmes, for example, Fuller and Unwin's studies of apprenticeship (2003a, 2003b) or institutional arrangements (e.g. Ramsden et al. 2004) within a specific country. Comparative studies within the UK tend to focus on specific differences in institutions or practices (e.g. Raffe

2000). While these types of separate analysis undoubtedly have value, the whole elephant remains obscure.

This chapter first presents an analytic framework for mapping 14–19 education policy, which focuses on the policy instruments that are used to shape policy. The framework is then used to compare recent policies related to vocational learning in the 14–19 age group. The chapter focuses on the policy instruments used in the four home countries, illustrating similarities and differences, and identifies potential shortcomings of those instruments used.[1] We argue that this framework is a useful tool for policy learning, as it provides a systematic way to think about the assumptions that underpin the choice of policy instruments and the possible ways that a policy might fail, and a common language for comparing policies across the home countries and beyond.

The policy instruments and institutions framework

Different analytical approaches may be taken to map the 14–19 policy scene. The framework presented here was adapted from analyses of the education and training system in the USA (McDonnell and Grubb 1991; Stasz and Bodilly 2004). It is also suitable to the UK case because both systems have high degrees of complexity and share a number of common characteristics.

The policy instruments and institutions framework (McDonnell and Grubb 1991) focuses on the instruments of public policy – the funding and regulatory mechanisms that different government levels use to shape and support activities – and on the institutions that provide education and training services. It has advantages as a comparative tool because it provides a systematic way of thinking about the assumptions that underpin different policy initiatives, and a common language for comparing policies across the home countries and beyond.

The framework includes four generic classes of policy instruments, each of which embodies a different set of assumptions about the policy problem to be addressed, the targets or recipients of the policy, the costs of policy implementation and who bears those costs.

Briefly, the classes of policy instruments to be examined are:

- **Mandates**: rules governing the actions of individual agencies, intended to produce compliance;

- **Inducements**: the transfer of money in return for certain actions, e.g. grants-in-aid to government agencies, private sector organisations and individuals;

- **Capacity-building**: the transfer of money for the purpose of longer-term investment in material, intellectual or human resources; and

- **Systems-changing**: the transfer of official authority among individuals and agencies to alter the system by which public goods and services are delivered (e.g. establishment of entirely new administrative structures, vouchers or addition of new providers).

In addition to these instruments, policy-makers may use **hortatory tools**, such as proclamations, speeches or public relations campaigns to exhort people to take the actions needed by the policy (Schneider and Ingram 1997). While these hortatory tools can support policy implementation, they do not carry the weight inherent in the four core instruments, which necessarily involve legislative backup.

The second key element in the framework is the set of institutions (public, private, within or outside the government) and programmes that provide services for the 14–19 age group. These institutions include secondary schools, further education (FE) colleges, universities, workplaces, learning centres, local Learning and Skills Councils (LLSCs), and Sector Skills Councils (SSCs). The programmes include, for example, the Apprenticeship scheme, New Deal, Increased Flexibilities in England, the Vocational Enhancement Programme in Northern Ireland, and Enterprise in Education in Scotland.

This framework also incorporates a set of descriptive categories (see Table 7.1), which elaborate the type of problem that a particular instrument may address and the assumptions that underlie the choice of a particular instrument. The framework categories provide a starting point for mapping 14–19 education policy that can be used to describe and compare the general policy environment as well as specific policy directives. A brief discussion of the categories follows.

1. Policy problem/purpose of policy

Policies are designed in a political environment shaped by ideology and interests, constituent pressures, and a variety of fiscal and institutional constraints. However, preferences are tempered by the need to reach compromises that ensure legislative commitment and by a variety of other constraints (e.g. availability of resources, competing demands of other policy areas).

2. Policy instruments

Any given policy may include multiple instruments. Policy-makers typically select a dominant instrument with others to supplement it. Most education and training policies include some form of inducement as the dominant policy instrument.

Inducements are often used if the policy goal is to produce a good that moves beyond a minimum standard or to encourage local institutions to assume new responsibilities. Inducements are also used if the policy problem is seen as the need to produce a good in a variety of different forms. This motive seems to underpin the

Table 7.1 Policy instruments and key assumptions

Instrument	Policy problem	Assumptions	
		Costs for initiators and recipients	Policy recipients and expected effects
Mandates	Undesirable behaviour or goods being produced. Lack of uniform standards.	Initiators: enforcement costs Recipients: compliance costs	Have capacity to comply; most will do so, though some shirking likely
Inducements	Valued goods or services not being produced with desired frequency	Initiators: direct oversight costs, slippage costs Recipients: opportunity costs, matching costs, excess costs	Have capacity to produce; money will elicit performance, though variability in production levels likely
Capacity-building	Lack of long-term investment in needed skills and valued goods	Initiators: direct oversight costs, slippage costs Recipients: opportunity costs, matching costs, excess costs	Currently lack capacity, but investment will mobilise it. Incentives will shift focus to longer-range goals. Pay-off is less likely and longer-term than for other instruments.
Systems-changing	Existing institutional arrangements are not producing desired results.	Initiators: transaction costs Recipients: loss of authority by established deliverers; start-up costs for new entrants	New entrants will produce desired results and will motivate established institution to improve. However, new entrants may generate a new set of problems.

Source: Adapted from McDonnell and Grubb (1991).

various policies that aim to provide 'choice' or 'options' (as in *14–19: Opportunity and excellence*, the 'Tomlinson proposals' and the 14–19 White Paper (DfES 2003; Working Group on 14–19 Reform 2004; DfES 2005)). Inducements are also used for system designs that permit variation in services, where it is desirable that policy implementation can respond to local conditions and needs.

The challenge with inducements – which produce variability by design – is to impose conditions on the receipt of funds in ways that promote the creativity and flexibility needed to promote high-quality outcomes but do not thwart intended policy goals.

The use of a capacity-building instrument assumes that the institutions lack capacity to produce the desired goods or are unable to do so quickly. The government makes a decision to invest funds that will reap benefits over the longer term. This type of instrument would be ideal for activities such as curriculum development, long-range follow-up, teacher professional development, etc., but often is not used.

Systems-changing policies are almost always used as a last resort when organisational norms and structures result in chronic unresponsiveness and inefficiency (i.e. when more stringent rules or more money will not help). Good examples in the education field are voucher programmes or the establishment of quasi-independent or private agencies to administer government programmes.

The most common strategy for balancing the diversity encouraged by inducement-based policies against the desire to ensure that specific targeting, service and performance goals are met is to impose mandates as conditions for receipt of the inducement. For example, new policies in higher education permit universities to charge top-up fees (inducement), but also require them to accept an access regulator to ensure equity in enrolments (mandate). Use of mandates and inducements in tandem assumes that the right incentives will work (either positively or negatively) to change behaviour and that policy-makers can obtain valid and reliable information about whether targets are performing.

Tools such as proclamations, speeches and public relations campaigns that exhort people to take the actions required for policy to succeed are widely evident. While these hortatory tools can be important for policy implementation, by creating a shared understanding and motivation to act, or by providing information, they do not carry the weight inherent in the other types of policy instruments just discussed, which necessarily involve legislative back-up (Schneider and Ingram 1997).

No instrument or suite of instruments will be entirely successful because recipients of the policy – individuals in need of education or training, firms wanting better trained workers, or public and private institutions providing education and training-related services – have interests of their own. In addition, as discussed further below, the broader policy context may affect policy implementation in unpredictable ways.

3. Assumptions (costs, targets and expected effects)

The cost assumptions outlined in Table 7.1 pertain to both the initiators and the recipients of policy. The government level initiating an inducement policy, for example, incurs **direct service costs** in the form of funds that are transferred to intended recipients. Funding grants usually have rules or regulations to ensure that the money is spent in a manner consistent with policy objectives. Regulations can create **oversight costs** or administrative expenses for monitoring. There may be **slippage costs** that occur when funds are siphoned into activities that have value for the targets – for example, if government funds are used to pay for services or activities that the local institution was already supporting. Some legislation may try to minimise slippage costs by imposing regulations that require recipients to use government funds to supplement but not supplant local revenues. Recipients may also incur costs even if they receive funding. They may incur opportunity costs, for example, if in producing services desired by the policy initiators they do not engage in other activities of importance to them or their constituents. Sometimes, inducement policies require recipients to make a financial commitment themselves, thus they incur a cost in the form of **matching funds**. Or recipients may incur **excess costs** if they spend more resources than they receive through the grant.

Policy-makers face two main challenges in selecting any of the four instruments: (1) they must estimate the costs that targets are willing to bear as precisely as possible, and (2) within these constraints, they must minimise their own costs and maximise the efficient use of resources. When recipients view costs differently policy-makers either will not be purchasing what they intended or will not obtain as much of it as they expected. In extreme cases recipients may determine that the costs are higher than potential benefits, and may opt out altogether (Stasz and Bodilly 2004).

4. Implementation context

According to the framework, the implementation context includes three elements: (1) choice of organisation to implement the policy, (2) interactions with other policies and organisational functions, and (3) exogenous social and economic conditions. The implementation context is basically defined by a set of variables that are largely independent of individual policy instruments and the assumptions underlying them, but whose interaction with different policies may be significant for explaining the ability of those policies to achieve their intended effects.

Policy-makers can significantly shape outcomes by their selection of institutions and government levels to further their policy goals. The characteristics of most significance are the goals and capacities of the implementing organisation – policy-makers must assess the capacity and the consistency of institutional norms with the expected effect of the policy.

Policy-makers must also take into account precursors, and how they may reinforce or constrain a new policy's intended effects. Furthermore, they must consider how they expect policies to co-ordinate (or not) with other policies.

Identifying relevant social and economic conditions and estimating their impact on particular policies are among the most difficult aspects of policy analysis. Estimates may include demographic changes, downswings or upturns in either national or regional economies, structures of local labour markets and conditions outside the country – policy-makers frequently have little direct influence over these conditions. Local policy-makers often lack the data and staff resources to take into account any but the most general demographic and economic trends.

5. Results and impact

With respect to outcomes, policy-makers begin with a set of expected outcomes or effects as illustrated in Table 7.1. In addition, once a policy has been implemented and evaluated, it is possible to track its actual effects, some of which may be unintended.

Policy-makers fine-tune their decisions as legislation is designed. As Table 7.1 partly indicates, these decisions often revolve around five issues:

- 'Who should be served?' specifies the policy recipients through such mechanisms as eligibility requirements.

- 'Who should pay?' determines the allocation of fiscal responsibility across governmental levels and agendas.

- 'What should be provided?' details the policy outputs – what kinds of education, training and other services should be provided and over what duration.

- 'Who should provide?' helps establish the context for

implementation by deciding which public or private institutions are authorised to provide services.

- 'What outcomes should be produced?' defines a policy's expected effects and establishes the standard by which its success will be judged by politicians and their constituents.

Design choices are not immutable and may change as problems are redefined and experience suggests the need for modification of a policy. Also, policies may emphasise different aspects – some care most about directing funds to particular recipients, while others are more concerned about the nature of services. Still other policies emphasise the level and type of outcomes.

How policies can fail

Why do some policies fail? The framework suggests three possible explanations for discrepancies among policy-makers' initial expectations, local implementation and effects. These explanations can be very useful for policy learning, as they enable a systematic, albeit *post hoc*, reflection on a particular policy's lack of impact. First, the problem may have been misdiagnosed. A policy problem that appears to stem from lack of investment may be due to a deeper structural problem that inhibits the ability to respond adequately. Policy-makers may make judgements based on poor data, or they may have deeply held beliefs that erroneously shape the way a policy problem is defined.

A second potential problem is a mismatch between the policy problem and the instrument. Policy-makers may rely on an instrument with a short time frame (e.g. an inducement) when a capacity-building approach is needed. The reason for this type of mismatch is often political – a capacity-building instrument tends to be less visible than other instruments, can be more expensive, and has a distant and uncertain pay-off.

Third, since the system of education and training is fragmented and decentralised, inconsistency in problem definition across policy actors and governmental levels is likely. At the national level, policy may be focused on special populations or interest groups or on promoting innovation. In contrast, local policy-makers may be focused on ongoing problems that affect all of their constituents. Policy at the national level may have a broad focus whereas local policy-makers may target specific groups. The various levels may have different beliefs about appropriateness of rules, or may operate under different incentive structures, constituent pressures and operating responsibilities.

The following section illustrates the framework by examining 14–19 vocational learning policies in England, Northern Ireland, Scotland and Wales. It would be impossible within the confines of this chapter to undertake a detailed analysis using every category in the policy and institutions framework, so this section focuses on policy instruments to indicate how the framework can be used in a comparative perspective.

14–19 vocational learning policy in the United Kingdom: policy context

The context in which vocational learning policy is formulated differs in each home nation. This context is influenced both by the history of education and training policy in each home country, and by the different terms of the 1999 devolution settlement. Scotland has the longest history of an education and training system separate from that in England, with the creation of distinctive educational institutions long before the devolution of administrative responsibilities and the creation of the Scotch Education Department in 1872. In Northern Ireland the Stormont government, established 1922, assumed substantial responsibilities for education and training (though this tradition of separate policy-making has been in abeyance for much of the last 30 years). The Welsh system of education has been tied more closely to that in England with the Welsh Office assuming responsibilities for education as late as 1970. Under the terms of the devolution settlement the Scottish Executive has legislative powers but Wales and Northern Ireland cannot pass legislation in this area (Finlay and Egan 2004; Byrne and Raffe 2005). The situation in Northern Ireland is further complicated by the suspension of devolved government since October 2002. Employment policy in all home nations is reserved to the Department of Work and Pensions (DWP) in London.

The governance arrangements and system of education and training providers in each home nation also vary. There is a complex system of governance bodies at different levels – with a UK-wide, national, regional or local remit – in each of England, Northern Ireland, Scotland and Wales, with some overlaps but also significant differences (Stasz and Wright 2004). There are also important differences between the institutions providing education and training for 14–19 year olds. Comprehensive schools are more widespread in Wales and Scotland than in England, and Northern Ireland has for many years had a system of selective admission at age 11 (Finlay and Egan 2004). In Scotland and Northern Ireland there is a clear division of labour between further education (FE) colleges and schools, with FE colleges having an almost entirely vocational remit, whereas in England and Wales there is more overlap. In the English context Sir Andrew Foster's review of FE colleges recommends a clearer 'economic mission' and a focus on 'vocational skills' (Foster 2005: 15). With this diversity it seems almost impossible to talk, administratively at least, of a 'UK-wide system'.

Likewise, the policy process in each home nation varies. Commentators (e.g. Finlay and Egan 2004) have noted a greater emphasis on consultative processes in post-devolution Scotland and Wales, and in Northern Ireland before devolved government was suspended, than in England. Wales and Scotland also appear to have a degree of stability in their political environment compared to England. Ruth Kelly, Secretary of State for Education in England at the time of writing, is the fourth in four years, whereas Jane Davidson, her counterpart as Assembly Minister for Education and Lifelong Learning has been in her present post for seven years.

Perhaps these different contexts and processes are reflected in the subtle differences in rhetoric and tone found in policy documents from the four countries. To generalise, the broad economic imperative for vocational learning, while found in documents from each home nation, is emphasised to the greatest extent in documents from England. Scottish documents place more emphasis on an entitlement to lifelong learning and citizenship, whereas in Welsh documents the stress is more on community regeneration and Welsh language and culture. The healing of divisions, as well as economic regeneration, is identified as a key purpose for education and training in Northern Ireland. Documents from Northern Ireland and Wales stress that they are finding their own solutions more than those from Scotland, perhaps reflecting the more recent break from English educational policy.

The final broad difference to note is that England, Northern Ireland, Scotland and Wales are at different 'stages' in developing 14–19 education policy. Wales has moved most quickly, and is now committed to implementing the Welsh Baccalaureate within the 'Learning Pathways' framework. A slower and more incremental approach has been adopted in England although commitment to a 14–19 phase has been signalled. 14–19 has only very recently become a feature of Scottish and Northern Irish policy debate (Raffe 2004).

However, the overall approach to vocational learning for 14–19 year olds, the main mechanisms utilised for reform, and the specific policy instruments used are more similar than different. Policy documents from each country, despite differences in rhetoric and tone, reveal a similar analysis of the central problems which vocational learning for 14–19 year olds must solve: economic and social. First, it is argued that low skill levels in the adult working population hamper economic performance and lead to skills gaps or shortages. This has been a mantra in policy documents for many years and recently reiterated in the Leitch review of UK skills (Leitch Review of Skills 2005). Vocational learning has been identified as an important way to attract more young people to continue into some form of post-compulsory education and training, and to gain the skills the economy needs. Second, vocational learning is (sometimes intentionally in policy, sometimes not as a policy intention but in practice) aimed at individuals who are not succeeding academically at school and deemed at risk of exclusion, in order to encourage them to gain the skills needed to progress to further education and training or skilled employment.

The home nations share broad policy trajectories, towards 'learner-centred' systems that are responsive to employer demand, with an emphasis on learner, parental and employer choice of courses (and, especially in England, choice of providers). These policy trajectories emphasise both competition between providers to raise standards, and co-operation between providers in order to ensure that students have access to a wide range of provision. There is potential for tension between collaboration and competition, and between learner and employer demands.[2]

Finally, 14–19 policy in each country has focused on changes to the curriculum and qualifications framework as a key mechanism for reform. Different solutions have been found: the unified Higher Still system for over-16s in Scotland; the Learning Pathways system of baccalaureate-style diplomas in Wales with 'work-focused experience' as part of the core (WAG 2003); the more restricted use of diplomas in England for vocational learning and for pupils who achieve five A*–C GCSEs including English and maths (DfES 2005); a curriculum entitlement which specifies a minimum number and range of subjects in Northern Ireland (PPRWG 2003).[3] However, the centrality of the qualification framework as a reform strategy is a notable feature of the UK 14–19 policy landscape.

14–19 vocational learning policy in the United Kingdom: policy instruments

This chapter will now focus on the policy instruments used in vocational learning policy for 14–19 year olds in the four countries of the UK. Table 7.2 provides further details for each country.[4] Even if there are significant differences in the policy history, context and process in England, Northern Ireland, Scotland and Wales, the key policy instruments used are remarkably similar. Inducements and hortatory tools are the most commonly used instruments. There is some capacity-building activity, although clear evidence of commitment to substantial long-term investment in material or human resources is rare. Beyond the end of compulsory education and training, strict mandates are very unusual. In England and Northern Ireland particularly new types of institutions have been introduced to provide education and training for 14–19 year olds, and the governance structure in all the home countries seems to be constantly shifting. However, there is little evidence at present of the wholesale transfer of powers from one set of organisations to another.

Some inducements are aimed at learners. For instance, the Educational Maintenance Allowance (a means-tested grant of up to £30 per week for 16–19 year olds in full-time education or training) has been introduced in all four countries. According to the DfES these 'have a proven track record in increasing participation' (DfES 2005: 6). Individual Learning Accounts have been reintroduced in Wales and Scotland but not in England and Northern Ireland. Wales also offers a means-tested Assembly Learning Grant to students in higher education (Higher Education Funding Council for Wales 2002). Some inducements are aimed at providers, such as funding for the Increased Flexibility Programme in England, the Vocational Enhancement Programme in Northern Ireland, and the Welsh Baccalaureate pilots. The Scottish Executive do not plan to use financial inducements of this type, but are opting instead for 'sustainable' funding for school/college activity through the Scottish

Table 7.2 The policies and institutions framework in the UK

	England	Northern Ireland	Scotland	Wales
Purpose of policy	Economic growth through higher level of skills in the population. Social inclusion Collaboration between providers so more options available to learners	Economic growth – especially filling skills gaps. Social inclusion. Healing divisions Collaboration between providers so more options available to learners	Economic growth. Social inclusion. Citizenship Collaboration between providers so more options available to learners	Economic growth. Social inclusion. Community regeneration and participation. Promotion of Welsh language and culture Collaboration between providers so more options available to learners
Policy instruments	Mostly inducements and hortatory policies. Some capacity-building to develop vocational diplomas though unclear whether long-term financial investment	Mostly inducements and hortatory policies. Three years funding for implementation of post-primary arrangements	Mostly inducements and hortatory policies. Three years funding for enterprise in education programme	Mostly inducements and hortatory policies. Capacity building (e.g. funding for 14–19 networks) but unclear how much funding or for how long
Assumptions	Costs: implementation and oversight costs for government, transaction costs for institutions (for collaborative provision), excess costs for institutions reported for Increased Flexibilities programme and some apprenticeship frameworks, opportunity costs for learners post-16 (in loss of potential earnings)	Costs as England. Vocational Enhancement Programme in pilot stage so unclear as yet if excess costs	Costs as England. Government strategy for vocational learning age 14–16 not yet out so not clear if excess costs	Costs as England. Institutions have reported excess costs in collaborative working and additional activities under 14–19 strategy

Recipients: institutions, learners, employers (encouraged to participate) Expected effects: increased participation post-16, progression to skilled employment or HE, improved attainment for those who do not currently achieve Level 2	Recipients: institutions, learners, employers (hortatory policy) Expected effects: fill specific skills gaps, support NI economic development	Recipients: institutions, learners, employers Expected effects: improved educational prospects for learners, transition to work or training	Recipients: institutions, learners, employers Expected effects: increased participation post-16, progression to skilled employment or HE, improved attainment for those who currently do not achieve basic skills or Level 2
Implementation context Implemented by: DfES and LSC, Sector Skills Councils for specialist diploma, QCA for qualification development, DWP for New Deal provision Interaction with: RDAs, CBI, employers, voluntary and community organisations – mechanisms unclear Skills strategy and exogenous conditions: Buoyant youth labour market in many areas a disincentive to participation post-16. General election 2005. Changing administrative and organisational structure, four education secretaries in four years	Implemented by: CCEA (curriculum and qualification development), Department of Education Northern Ireland and Department of Education and Learning Northern Ireland, DWP for New Deal Provision Interaction with: employers, skills strategy for Northern Ireland; consultation on role of Further Education Exogenous conditions: currently under direct rule but emphasis on right solution for Northern Ireland	Implemented by: Scottish Executive Education Department, Education, Transport and Lifelong Learning Department, DWP for New Deal provision, LEAs, Local Enterprise Companies for work-based learning Interaction with: Scottish Enterprise, Lifelong Enterprise, learning strategy, Enterprise strategy Exogenous conditions: devolution settlement, history of separate education system, access to learning a problem in rural areas	Implemented by: Welsh Assembly Government (Education and Lifelong Learning department), ELWa, 14–19 networks at local level, ACCAC and WJEC for curriculum and qualifications development, DWP for New Deal provision. Emphasis on interaction with voluntary and community organisations Interaction with Skills and Employment Action Plan Exogenous conditions: high levels of economic inactivity in parts of Wales, post-devolution emphasis on 'Welsh solution'

Table 7.2 The policies and institutions framework in the UK (continued)

	England	Northern Ireland	Scotland	Wales
Results and impact	Evidence limited. Too early to tell impact of vocational learning for 14–16s on attainment in examinations at 16, though benefits in motivation and social skills reported. Ofsted reports poor quality teaching and assessment widespread Difficult to secure employer engagement in delivery of vocational learning	Evidence limited, still in early policy formation and development stage Difficult to secure employer engagement in delivery of vocational learning	Evidence that Higher Still policies have not halted 'academic drift'. 14–19 policy in very early stages, mainly focused on vocational learning for 14–16 year olds Difficult to secure employer engagement in delivery of vocational learning	Evidence limited. Emerging evidence from Welsh Bacc. pilots: pupil enjoyment of broader curriculum experience, but response of HE and employers mixed Difficult to secure employer engagement in delivery of vocational learning

Abbreviations used in this table (in order of appearance) are as follows: HE, higher education; NI, Northern Ireland; DfES, Department for Education and Skills; LSC, Learning and Skills Council; QCA, Qualifications and Curriculum Authority; DWP, Department of Work and Pensions; RDAs, Regional Development Agencies; CBI, Confederation of British Industry; CCEA, Council for the Curriculum, Examinations and Assessment; LEAs, local education authorities; ELWa, Education and Learning Wales; ACCAC, Awdurdod Cymwysterau, Cwricwlwm ac Asesu Cymru (Qualifications, Curriculum and Assessment Authority for Wales); WJEC, Welsh Joint Education Committee.

Further Education Funding Council that would augment funding for schools (£41.5m of additional resources over the financial years 2005/06 and 2006/07) (Scottish Executive 2005).

Hortatory tools are also common across the UK. Hortatory tools are frequently aimed at employers: this is the main approach to employer engagement in vocational learning for 14–19 year olds in each country. Plans for vocational learning for 14–19 year olds assume substantial input from employers: providing placements for work experience, enterprise education and work-based learning; sometimes designing programmes and qualifications; working in partnership with providers and governance bodies to plan and organise aspects of 14–19 provision. However, policy documents suggest that nothing stronger than encouragement will be used to secure this engagement and input. The DfES promise to 'work with employers to offer more opportunities to young people to learn at work and outside school' (DfES 2005: 50); Education and Learning Wales (ELWa) recommend a redesign of Modern Apprenticeship frameworks in order to 'encourage better employer engagement with apprenticeship programmes' (ELWa 2004: 28); the Scottish Executive plan to 'encourage greater involvement from the business community' in their strategy to promote enterprise through education (Scottish Executive 2004a: 7).

The targets of hortatory policy can be more wide-ranging. For instance, the publicity campaign for the Welsh Baccalaureate – advertising, presentations and seminars, student conferences – aims to promote the qualification to learners and providers, and to end-users (employers and universities).

Policy documents in all four countries often talk about developing or building capacity. However, clear evidence of capacity-building as defined in the framework – a commitment to long-term and large-scale investment in developing goods, facilities, personnel – is rare. Specific funds have been allocated for the medium term in Scotland and Northern Ireland. Additional resources of £20m have been secured for implementing the new post-primary arrangements in Northern Ireland over the next three years. Detailed decisions on distribution will be devolved to the local level, but it is envisaged that this funding will support the curriculum entitlement framework and collaboration between schools and colleges.[5] In Scotland new vocational qualifications for pupils aged 14–16 are being developed and piloted by the Scottish Qualifications Authority (SQA) with a view to national roll-out in 2007–8, and the Executive has devoted £44m from 2003–6 for Enterprise in Education (£32m of which has been devolved to local authorities) and £41.5m across the financial years 2005/06 and 2006/07 to support school pupils' learning in FE colleges (Scottish Executive 2004b, 2004c, 2005).

ELWa in their Workplace Learning Review recommend the expansion of provider capacity to offer vocational provision from 14 onwards, but how this will be done and how much will be committed are not specified (ELWa 2004). The Welsh Assembly Government (WAG) has made available a £50,000 grant for each 14–19 Network for the financial year 2004–5, a further £140,000 across Wales to be match-funded locally for learning coach and personal support pilot work, and it has proposed an unspecified amount for 'capacity-building' in community participation and work-focused experience (WAG 2004). It is not clear how long this sort of investment will last. In England some money will be available for improving facilities in schools through the Building Schools for the Future Programme (DfES 2004). The DfES also plan to 'increase the capacity of the education system to offer vocational education' in both schools and colleges. The 14–19 White Paper recognises the need for development work for the new specialised diplomas, and for staff development to enable school teachers to deliver vocational learning (DfES 2005: 76). However, there is less clarity on how this development work is to be funded.

Whereas most pilot funding is short term and has a short lead-in time, institutions involved in the Welsh Baccalaureate pilot were funded for one year's planning prior to introducing the qualification. This sort of capacity-building in a pilot programme is very unusual, but evaluations of 14–19 Pathfinders and the Increased Flexibility Programme reveal that without lead-in time institutions involved can struggle with planning and implementation (Golden *et al.* 2004; Higham *et al.* 2004; Ofsted 2004).

There is little evidence of significant systems-changing in the governance and power structures of 14–19 education and training in any of the home countries at present, though these structures are constantly shifting.[6] The landscape of providers of 14–19 education and training in Wales and Scotland appears relatively stable at present, although existing providers are being required to undertake new tasks (such as FE colleges providing vocational learning for 14–16 year olds). In England on the other hand, new and increasingly specialised types of providers are constantly being introduced. Recent policy places much of the onus for offering vocational provision for 14–19 year olds on specialist schools with the appropriate specialisms (part of a greatly expanded network of specialist schools), Centres of Vocational Excellence, and a new network of skills academies (DfES 2005; DfES *et al.* 2005). Specialist schools are being introduced in Northern Ireland, where the Department for Employment and Learning (DELNI) are also considering structural change in the FE sector (moving to a smaller number of larger units). The organisational structure of secondary education will be fundamentally altered with the abolition of selection at age 11 in 2008 (DENI 2004; DELNI 2004).

Strict legal mandates – which compel individuals, institutions or employers to do something or risk being penalised – are uncommon compared to other European countries. There is the generalised legal requirement of compulsory education to age 16. Also, some curriculum requirements relate to vocational education: for instance a statutory requirement to deliver work-related learning at Key Stage 4 was introduced in England in September 2004, and 'Learning for Life and Work' will be made a compulsory part of the post-primary curriculum in Northern Ireland in Autumn 2006 (CCEA 2004).

Mandates are very rare beyond the end of compulsory education and training. In England there are employer levies for training in two sectors – construction and electrical engineering. However, in England and the other home countries there are almost no mechanisms to compel employers to provide or pay for vocational learning. The Republic of Ireland provides a useful point of comparison. Under the Education (Welfare) Act 2000, any individuals under 18 who left school without adequate qualifications must register with the National Educational Welfare Board (NEWB) to engage in a programme of training if they wish to gain employment, and employers can only employ under-18s who have registered with the NEWB (NEWB 2005). The equivalent in England is the weaker instrument of a 'right to paid time off work' to study or train for approved qualifications for 16–17 year olds not qualified to Level 2.[7]

Also, it is assumed that employers will become involved in the work-related and vocational learning programmes under development but there are few instruments to compel them to do so. Evaluations of the 14–19 Pathfinders and Increased Flexibility programmes in England and policy documents on enterprise education in Scotland indicate that employer involvement is variable and often weak (Golden *et al.* 2004, 2005; Higham *et al.* 2004; Scottish Executive 2003b, 2004a). The most recent *Learning Pathways 14–19 Guidance* in Wales hints at the possible use of some weak form of mandate: the Assembly will consider whether organisations in receipt of public funds should in future be required to support work-focused experience developments (WAG 2004). This suggestion falls short of the clear mandates used outside the UK.

There are also few strict mandates on providers. Rather, the Government uses inspection and funding regimes and performance targets as steering and somewhat weak accountability mechanisms. Inspections and particularly funding tied to inspections can be used as instruments for accountability. For instance, in England the

Learning and Skills Council can deny funding to institutions deemed to be underperforming in their inspections, and has done so on several occasions, but whether or not to exercise this power is left to the discretion of individual inspectors.[8] Likewise, schools placed in 'special measures' by Ofsted can have certain powers of autonomy removed. Even in the absence of strict mandates, providers report feeling under pressure and compelled to perform or act in certain ways. So although these mechanisms are not as strict as the regulatory mandates defined within the framework, and perhaps not as strong as policy-makers would like, they can still exert pressure to comply (Hodgson *et al.* 2005a).

Another possible steering mechanism is directing funding at provision that relates explicitly to government priorities. This has been utilised most clearly in Northern Ireland, where funding for expanding FE provision aims to fill skills gaps (DELNI 2004). The Scottish Executive on the other hand has rejected the strategy of addressing sectoral and occupational shortages through differential levels of funding (Scottish Executive 2003a).

Concluding commentary: impact of current 14–19 vocational learning policy

It is difficult to comment on the impact or results of current developments in 14–19 vocational learning policy in England, Northern Ireland, Scotland and Wales. Many of these policies are relatively new, and still in their 'design' or 'pilot' stages. However, one key problem that seems to be emerging is that too little attention is paid to significant issues of capacity. Inducement and hortatory policies, which rest on the assumption that capacity is already in place, are common, but long-term and substantial investment in building capacity is not. However, there is growing evidence in all home countries that the required capacity is not currently present. For instance, the lack of work-based provision in many areas and lack of employers willing to provide placements has been noted as a problem by 14–19 Pathfinders in England and 14–19 Networks in Wales (Higham *et al.* 2004; Williams 2005). Teacher capacity is likely to become an increasingly important issue, particularly if plans to teach 14–16 year olds in colleges and run more vocational courses (including specialised diplomas) in schools are to be rolled out fully.

Furthermore, current vocational learning policy for 14–19 year olds in all home countries rests on the assumption that providers will collaborate to offer a wide range of learning opportunities. Evaluations indicate that collaborative working requires careful administration and co-ordination, and incurs high costs (time and money), but much of the funding for collaboration is short-term (Hodgson *et al.* 2005b).

The implications of some of these developments do not appear to have been fully thought through. The over-reliance on inducement-type strategies, which are not backed up by strong accountability, is not a recipe for the types of reforms that policy-makers and stakeholders seem to want.

A framework for comparing policies, such as the one provided here, could contribute to policy learning and perhaps more thoughtful policy-making, as it can reveal the assumptions that lie behind the choice of policy instruments. As this analysis has shown, policy stemming from the wrong assumptions has less chance of success. Furthermore, the use of policy instruments may be an important area for research, as their use and nature has changed over time, and understanding this history may contribute to further policy learning.

Notes

1. This chapter is developed from research funded by the Learning and Skills Research Centre (LSRC) on the project 'Modelling a vocational learning system for the 21st century'.

2. For example it was found that students sometimes do not wish to take the courses in priority skills areas, which the Department for Employment and Learning Northern Ireland (DELNI) encourages colleges to focus on (DELNI 2003).

3. A minimum entitlement of 24 courses at Key Stage 4 and 27 courses post-16 was recommended. One-third of these courses should be vocational.

4. Table 7.2 is inevitably biased towards policy development in England and Wales, reflecting the lack of a 14–19 discourse until recently in Scotland and Northern Ireland. Scottish and Northern Irish policies do not fit tidily into a 14–19 frame.

5. Mr Gardiner, Secretary of State of Education for Northern Ireland, written answer in response to parliamentary question 27 January 2005. Hansard Col. 510W. Online. Available HTTP: http://www.publications.parliament.uk/pa/cm/cmhansrd.htm (accessed 1 March 2005).

6. In England major restructuring took place from 2001–03 with the Learning and Skills Council, Regional Development Agencies, Sector Skills Councils and other bodies. Some (although less major) restructuring took place at a similar time in the other home countries. More fundamental systems changing took place in Wales in 2006 when the Welsh Development Agency, Wales Tourist Board and ELWa were merged with their sponsor departments and became part of the Welsh Assembly Government (WAG 2005).

7. Online. Available HTTP: http://www.dfes.gov.uk/tfst (accessed 5 March 2005).

8. However, in his review of FE colleges Sir Andrew Foster calls for a stricter regime with colleges judged to be 'failing' to be given 12 months to improve before being taken over by other colleges or closed (Foster 2005).

References

Byrne, D. and Raffe, D. (2005) *Establishing a UK 'Home International' Comparative Research Programme for Post-compulsory Learning*. Learning and Skills Research Centre (LSRC) Report. London: Learning and Skills Development Agency (LSDA).

Council for the Curriculum, Examinations and Assessment (CCEA) (2004) 'GCSEs and A levels remain top class qualifications'. Press release 18 Oct 2004. Online. Available HTTP: http://www.rewardinglearning.com/development/new/press/2004/press_181004.html (accessed 1 March 2005).

Department for Employment and Learning Northern Ireland (DELNI) (2003) *Department for Employment and Learning Evaluation of Further Education Funding. Final report*. Belfast: DELNI.

— (2004) *Further Education Means Business*. Belfast: DELNI.

Department of Education Northern Ireland (DENI) (2004) 'Education Minister emphasises "Standards, not structures", as he announces new "real-world skills" curriculum'. Press release 23 June 2004. Online. Available HTTP: http://www.deni.gov.uk/de_news/press_releases/june_04/23.06.04.htm (accessed 1 March 2005).

Department for Education and Skills (DfES) (2003) *14–19: Opportunity and excellence*. Norwich: HMSO.

— (2004) *Five Year Strategy for Children and Learners*. London: DfES.

— (2005) *14–19 Education and Skills*. London: DfES.

DfES, DTI, DWP, HMT (2005) *Skills: Getting on in business, getting on at work*. London: HMSO.

Education and Learning Wales (ELWa) (2004) *Developing the Workforce – Learning in and for the workplace. Final report*. Cardiff: ELWa.

Finlay, I. and Egan, D. (2004) 'What policy trajectories are the national governments in England, Wales, Northern Ireland and Scotland following and are they converging or diverging? – A comparative perspective'. Working Paper WP20, Nuffield 14–19 Review. Online. Available HTTP: http://www.nuffield14–19review.org.uk/documents/shtml (accessed 20 February 2005).

Foster, A. (2005) *Realising the Potential. A review of the future role of further education colleges*. Nottingham: DfES.

Fuller, A. and Unwin, L. (2003a) 'Creating a "Modern Apprenticeship": a critique of the UK's multi-sector, social inclusion approach'. *Journal of Education and Work*, 16 (1), 5–26.

— (2003b) 'Learning as apprentices in the contemporary UK workplace: creating and managing expansive and restrictive participation'. *Journal of Education and Work*, 16 (4), 407–26.

Golden, S., Nelson, J., O'Donnell, L. and Morris, M. (2004) *Evaluation of Increased Flexibilities for 14–16 year olds: The first year.* DfES Research Report RR511. Nottingham: DfES.

Golden, S., O'Donnell, L. and Rudd, P. (2005) *Evaluation of Increased Flexibility of 14–16 year olds Programme: The second year.* DfES Research Report RR609. Nottingham: DfES.

Higham, J., Haynes, G., Wragg, C. and Yeomans, D. (2004) *14–19 Pathfinders: An evaluation of the first year.* Leeds, Exeter: University of Leeds, University of Exeter.

Higher Education Funding Council for Wales (2002) *Assembly Learning Grants.* Circular WO2/41HE. Cardiff: Higher Education Funding Council for Wales.

Hodgson, A., Spours, K., Coffield, F., Steer, R., Finlay, I., Edward, S. and Gregson, M. (2005a) *A New Learning and Skills Landscape? The LSC within the learning and skills sector.* ESRC TLRP project 'Impact of policy on learning and inclusion' Research Report 1. Institute of Education, University of London.

Hodgson, A., Spours, K. and Wright, S. (2005b) 'From collaborative initiatives to a coherent 14–19 phase? Institutional dimensions of 14–19 education and training in England'. A seminar discussion paper for the Nuffield 14–19 Review. Paper presented at 'The institutional dimension of 14–19 reform in England: Seminar 1' held at the Nuffield Foundation, London, 28 February 2005.

Leitch Review of Skills (2005) *Skills in the UK: The long-term challenge. Interim report.* London: HMSO.

McDonnell, L.M. and Grubb, W.N. (1991) *Education and Training for Work: The policy instruments and the institutions.* R-4026-NCRVE/UCB. Santa Monica: RAND Corporation.

National Educational Welfare Board (NEWB) (2005) *Frequently Answered Questions.* Online. Available HTTP: http://www.newb.ie/faqs.shtml (accessed 1 March 2005).

Ofsted (2004) *Increased Flexibility Programme at Key Stage 4: Evaluation of the first year.* London: Ofsted.

Post-Primary Review Working Group (PPRWG) (2003) *Future Post-primary Arrangements in Northern Ireland. Advice from the Post-Primary Review Working Group.* The Costello Report. Belfast: DENI.

Raffe, D. (2000) 'Investigating the education systems of the United Kingdom'. *Oxford Studies in Comparative Education*, 9 (2), 9–28.

Raffe, D. (2004) 'Aims and purposes: philosophical issues'. Working Paper WP2, Nuffield 14–19 Review. Online. Available HTTP: www.nuffield14–19review.org.uk/documents/shtml (accessed 20 February 2005).

Ramsden, M., Bennett, R.J. and Fuller, C. (2004) 'Short-term policy and the changing institutional landscape of post-16 education and training: the case of learning partnerships in England, Scotland, and Wales'. *Journal of Education and Work*, 17 (2), 139–65.

Schneider, A.L. and Ingram, H. (1997) *Policy Design for Democracy*. Lawrence, Kansas: University Press of Kansas.

Scottish Executive (2003a) *Life through Learning: Learning through life. The lifelong learning strategy for Scotland*. Edinburgh: Enterprise, Transport and Lifelong Learning Department.

— (2003b) *Determined to Succeed: Enterprise in education. Scottish Executive response*. Edinburgh: Scottish Executive.

— (2004a) *Determined to Succeed One Year On*. Edinburgh: Scottish Executive.

— (2004b) *Life through Learning: Learning through Life. The lifelong learning strategy for Scotland strategy update*. Edinburgh: Scottish Executive.

— (2004c) *Building the Foundations of a Lifelong Learning Society. Interim report*. Edinburgh: Scottish Executive.

— (2005) *Lifelong Partners. Scotland's schools and colleges building the foundations of a lifelong learning society. A strategy for partnership*. Edinburgh: Scottish Executive.

Stasz, C. and Bodilly, S. (2004) *Efforts to Improve the Quality of Vocational Education in Secondary Schools: Impact of federal and state policies*. MR-1655-USDE. Santa Monica: RAND Corporation. Online. Available HTTP: www.rand.org/publications/MR/MR1655 (accessed 17 September 2006).

Stasz, C. and Wright, S. (2004) *Emerging Policy for Vocational Learning in England. Will it lead to a better system?* London: Learning and Skills Research Centre. Online. Available HTTP: http://lsda.org.uk/files/PDF/1657.pdf (accessed 17 September 2006).

Welsh Assembly Government (WAG) (2003) *Learning Country: Learning Pathways Action Plan*. Cardiff: WAG.

— (2004) *Learning Country: Learning Pathways 14–19 Guidance*. National Assembly for Wales circular No: 37/2004. Cardiff: WAG.

— (2005) *Skills and Employment Action Plan for Wales 2005.* Cardiff: WAG.

Williams, J. (2005) 'Building a 14–19 learning pathways network'. Paper presented at Nuffield Review seminar '14–19 education in Wales', University of Cardiff, 25 January 2005.

Working Group on 14–19 Reform (2004) *14–19 Curriculum and Qualifications Reform: Final report.* London: DfES.

8 Creating 'political space' for policy learning in 14–19 education and training in England

Ann Hodgson and Ken Spours

Introduction

The publication of the *14–19 Education and Skills* White Paper (DfES 2005a) in February 2005 marked the end of a three-year period of intense public debate about the nature of 14–19 education and training in England. What began in 2002 as a conventional government-led consultation process around the Green Paper, *14–19 Education: Extending opportunities, raising standards* (DfES 2002), ended in a bitter political and media battle about the abolition of GCSEs and A levels. In between, there was a crisis around A level marking; two high-level resignations (a minister and the chief executive of a government agency); the meteoric rise to power of a young politician, David Miliband, associated with radical curriculum unification ideas; and the establishment of a high-profile independent Working Party on 14–19 Curriculum and Qualifications Reform, chaired by a former Chief Inspector, Mike Tomlinson, and involving thousands of young people, researchers, practitioners and policy-makers in the discussion of a unified 14–19 diploma system (Working Group on 14–19 Reform 2004). Meanwhile, at the local level, building on their past experience, local education authorities (LEAs), the newly formed local Learning and Skills Councils (LLSCs), schools, colleges and work-based learning providers in many areas of the country began to develop Tomlinson-inspired unified 14–19·

plans. Then, in February 2005, with the publication of the 14–19 White Paper, the Government rejected the central proposal of the Tomlinson Final Report – a unified diploma system – by announcing its decision to retain GCSEs and A levels and to focus reform once again on changes to vocational qualifications through the development of new specialised diplomas. This is a strategy that has been tried on a number of occasions in the past (e.g. the development of the Certificate of Pre-Vocational Education (CPVE), the Diploma of Vocational Education (DVE) and General National Vocational Qualifications (GNVQs)), but has not managed to achieve successive administrations' aims of raising levels of participation and attainment to match or exceed those of competitor countries.

As this brief history of recent policy activity illustrates, 14–19 education and training in England constitutes a particularly difficult terrain for policy-making and, we will argue, for policy learning. While the media frenzy that followed the publication of the 14–19 White Paper has died down, the public debate about the aims, purposes, shape and organisation of the 14–19 phase rumbles on (e.g. Hayward *et al.* 2005) with no clear consensus between practitioners, policy-makers and researchers.

The difficulties of policy-making in this area can partly be explained by the inherently complex nature of 14–19 education and training: it straddles compulsory and post-compulsory education, full-time learning and working life and involves a wide range of qualifications, different types of institutions and learning environments. Several different teams of civil servants and ministers within the Department for Education and Skills (DfES) thus have a stake in 14–19 policy-making and the individual and combined effects of their actions ripple out across a wide area sometimes in a contradictory fashion. It is also a contested arena. While the concept of a 14–19 phase is relatively new in terms of official national policy discourse – it first received serious attention in the 2002 Green Paper *14–19 Education: Extending opportunities, raising standards* (DfES 2002) – it has been part of wider educational professional discourse and lived experience since the introduction of the Technical and Vocational Education Initiative (TVEI) in the late 1980s. The vision of an inclusive and unified phase, originating in *A British Baccalaureate* (Finegold *et al.* 1990), but building on the professional experience of educating 14–19 year olds, gradually emerged and took hold throughout that decade, but existed alongside the reality of an increasingly divided triple-track post-16 national qualifications system (Hodgson and Spours 2003). These different unofficial and official visions for the development of the phase are manifest in the Tomlinson Final Report (Working Group on 14–19 Reform 2004), on the one hand, and the Government's 14–19 White Paper and its Implementation Plan (DfES 2005a, 2005b) on the other.

In this contested terrain, political considerations in policy-making predominate and the views of the education profession appear to be marginalised. The role of policy memory to reap the benefits of the long gestation period of professional thinking about 14–19 education and training seems to have made little impact on the higher levels of policy-making. The main risk is that the Government will pursue a strategy on vocational education that may not fully learn from past experience and failure. Moreover, because the policy process itself is being conducted within politically determined timescales – witness the rush to develop all 14 specialised diploma lines at Foundation, Intermediate and Advanced Level by 2010 (DfES 2005b) – policy-makers appear unwilling to listen seriously to the problems raised by practitioners who will have to implement the reforms. This latter point has particular significance within the English system because of the tradition of bottom-up innovation in this area.

Taking these developments and issues as its context, this chapter attempts to develop an analytical framework to understand the nature of policy-making and issues of policy learning in 14–19 curriculum and qualifications reform in England. The framework, which comprises the inter-related dimensions of 'political eras'; 'the education state'; 'the policy process'; and 'political space', is used in three ways. First, it is employed as an explanatory device for narrating 14–19 developments in England over the last 20 years. In attempting to make sense of this complex and contested landscape, we hope to develop an account that can be shared between policy-makers, practitioners and researchers. Second, the framework can be regarded as a set of tools to identify why and where problems of policy learning occur. Finally, we look at ways in which one of the dimensions – political space – might be developed to support the interaction of policy-makers, practitioners and researchers in a more deliberative policy-making process (Hajer and Wagenaar 2003). We argue that this kind of policy-making, which has the potential to harness the different strengths and experiences of these three key actors, is more likely to lead to a climate in which policy learning can thrive and inform the policy process.

A changed policy landscape

Problems of policy-making and policy learning in 14–19 education and training have been affected not only by the specificities of this phase but also by seismic shifts in the general policy landscape. Education policy-making in England has changed dramatically since the 1944 Education Act with its relatively straightforward model of a tripartite balance of power between national government, LEAs and education providers – each playing its own particular part in the translation of policy into practice (Ball 1997). Chapter 1 of this volume characterised this approach as demonstrating features of the 'rational' model of policy-making. Over the last 50 years, however, there has been a move towards a more complex and 'politicised' model of governance, resulting from a fundamental economic, political and ideological disturbance of post-war arrangements. This new model stems primarily from the policies associated with the 18 years of Conservative rule in the 1980s and 1990s, but many of its features have been honed under consecutive New Labour administrations (Clarke *et al.* 2000; Phillips and Furlong 2001).

It is possible to identify at least five major inter-related changes in the policy-making process that date back to the mid-1970s but which have, arguably, continued or even accelerated during the period since New Labour came into power in 1997.

The growth of 'arm's-length' agencies

The last 20 years have seen a growing role for quasi-autonomous non-governmental organisations (quangos) or non-departmental public bodies (NDPBs) in policy-making and policy enactment. In the post-compulsory field examples include the Learning and Skills Council (LSC), Ofsted, the Adult Learning Inspectorate (ALI), the Qualifications and Curriculum Authority (QCA) as well as the Adult Basic Skills Strategy Unit (ABSSU) and the Post-16 Teaching and Learning Standards Unit inside the DfES.

The quasi-market in education and arm's-length steering mechanisms

New Labour, as part of a wider public sector modernisation agenda, has perpetuated a quasi-market in education (Du Gay 2000; Newman 2000) which aims to increase autonomy for individual education providers, to stimulate the introduction of new private providers, and to encourage parents and learners to see themselves as consumers of public services (DfES 2005c). At the same time, marketisation has been accompanied by the use of powerful national steering mechanisms as a form of accountability and to retain central political leverage in what could have become a much more devolved system (Hodgson *et al.* 2005).

A plethora of policy texts

The traditional texts of government (e.g. White Papers, Acts of Parliament and influential reports by government commissions) have been joined by a veritable flood of different types of policy documents from both central government and its agencies. There are 'next steps' documents, strategy documents, consultation documents, curriculum documents, guidance documents and so on. Moreover, lifelong learning policy documents are no longer simply the preserve of one government department – the Department for Trade and Industry, the Department for Work and Pensions, the Treasury and the Cabinet Office are increasingly involved alongside the DfES.

Devolution and double devolution

Devolution of powers to the Welsh Assembly and the Scottish Parliament in the latter part of the 20th century means that the UK now has at least three types of education systems within it, each of which has somewhat different policy-making processes, with the potential for policy analysts to use the tool of 'home international' comparison (Raffe, 2005). At the same time, David Miliband, the Minister for Communities and Local Government, has been arguing for a 'double devolution' from national government to local government and from local government to communities (Miliband 2006a).

Political centralisation and politicisation

While the first four changes set out so far suggest that the policy landscape has become much more complex and unpredictable, the Government has developed new mechanisms to assert central political control. Under New Labour an army of political advisers has been drafted into key government departments with a major role for the Prime Minister's Policy Unit in ministerial and departmental policy-making.

The case for a new analytical framework for policy-making and policy learning

These five changes have resulted in a movement away from a rational/bureaucratic model of policy-making towards a new form of governance in England that Chapter 1 describes as a predominantly 'politicised' model. This shift has profound consequences for policy-making and policy learning and, we argue, requires a new analytical framework for understanding 14–19 education and training.

First, we have to be able to understand why there has been so much reform without much change. In our view, this demands a historical perspective on the policy process and the promotion of policy learning, so that mistakes from the past are not repeated. Our response is the first dimension of the framework – 'political eras' – informed by the concept of 'policy memory'. Second, increased powers for central government, on the one hand, and individual educational institutions, on the other, have hollowed out the role of local governance (LGA 2004), posing questions about the nature of the education state in the early 21st century. Hence, we have the 'education state' as the second dimension of our framework to allow us to reflect on its role in policy learning. The third dimension – 'the policy process' – needs to be viewed within the dynamics of this reconfigured education state and has to be able to explain the increased complexity of policy-making and its implications for policy learning. Finally, we are interested in the possibilities of interventions in the policy process, which provide opportunities for policy learning. We, therefore, use the concept of 'political space' as the final tool within the analytical framework.

A framework of analysis for 14–19 education policy

This analytical policy framework builds on the work of Bowe *et al.* (1992) by placing their concept of a policy triangle within an historical, political and state context (see Figure 8.1). Each of these tools is applied to 14–19 education and training policy and comments made on aspects of policy learning.

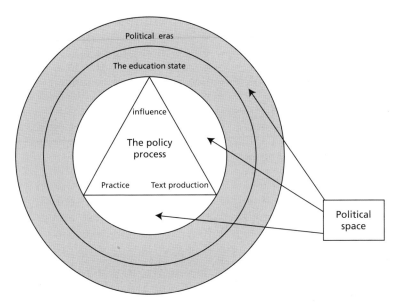

Figure 8.1 An analytical policy framework

Dimension 1. Political eras

Policy analysts, when describing policy-makers' inability to learn from the past in relation to 14–19 reform, have commented on their tendency to suffer from 'policy amnesia' (Higham *et al.* 2002; Higham and Yeomans 2005 and Chapter 2 of this volume). We would contend that this condition is caused by a short political cycle dominated by the politics of general elections and by the rapid turnover of ministerial teams and political advisers, which prevents the building of 'policy memory', together with the politicisation of education policy and particularly policies involving high-stakes examinations such as GCSEs and A levels. Policy amnesia is compounded by a lack of trust in the education profession with its 'grounded' memory of what has worked in particular contexts.

In recognition of the importance of policy memory and learning from the past, we have developed the term 'political era' to provide a historical and wider contextual analysis for interpreting policy-making trends and particular 'moments' in the education policy process. In its broadest sense a 'political era' might be defined as a fundamental shift in relationships between social classes, the state and markets and how people see themselves as citizens and consumers (Clarke and Newman 2004). In this chapter, where we are considering education policy and the 14–19 phase in particular, we use the term 'political era' as a period of politics and policy-making framed by three major factors: underlying societal shifts and historical trends which affect the 'shape' of the education and training system; dominant political ideology which affects the parameters for reform; and national and international education debates which either support or contest the dominant ideology. In terms of 14–19 education and training, we have argued elsewhere that the period from the mid-1980s to the present, despite changes in governments, broadly constitutes a single political era which has been dominated by three fundamental ideas: selective approaches to curriculum and qualifications policy, articulated through the academic/vocational divide; the belief in markets and institutional competition; and labour market voluntarism (Hodgson and Spours 2004).

The concept of 'political era' can assist with an understanding of the 14–19 policy process and the issue of policy learning in a number of ways. First, it provides an explanation of reform without change or what Lumby and Foskett (Chapter 4 this volume) refer to as 'adaptive behaviour', in which policy-makers try to correct a problem without exploring its roots. As part of adaptive behaviour, policy learning is about the selection of solutions within confined policy parameters that conform to the dominant ideology of the political era. Second, a political era may reflect what Steinberg and Johnson (2004) term the politics of 'passive revolution', in which the aim of limited reform is to head off the possibility of more radical change. Policy learning as part of passive revolution is a calculation designed to appropriate politically aspects of radical programmes while placing these within a conservative logic. This is essentially what the 14–19 White Paper did with the Tomlinson proposals for a unified 14–19 curriculum and qualifications system. Third, the persistence of a political era may be aided by ideological reinvention. New Labour has re-articulated Conservative ideas of new public management through its public service 'modernisation' agenda (Newman 2000), leading to a common template for reform applied across different public services. This generalised approach to reform can easily result in policy dogma because of the belief, in this particular case, that the quasi-market approach to health reform can be creatively applied to education. Policy learning is thus focused narrowly on policy borrowing from other public service areas, rather than on learning from traditions within education itself, the latter being associated with old-style professionalism and anti-modernisation.

Attempts by politicians to historically extend a political era, either for ideological or more politically pragmatic reasons, leads to what we have termed the 'politicisation' of policy, in which solutions are selected according to the extent they support the dominant political project. At the same time, however, the internal dynamics of the political era also generate an alternative set of national and international debates and blueprints. In the case of 14–19 education and training, proposals emerged for a more unified and inclusive approach to expanding upper secondary education systems (Lasonen and Young 1998). In England, as we have seen, these ideas can be traced back to the publication of *A British Baccalaureate* (Finegold *et al.* 1990), together with many other unification proposals throughout the 1990s (Hodgson and Spours 2003). More recently, unification ideas moved to a more prominent position in national policy debates, culminating in the Tomlinson Final Report (Working Group on 14–19 Reform 2004). The unified concept of a 14–19 phase could be seen as a desire to bring to an end a political era of upper secondary education dominated by Conservative market-led and divisive ideology and to open up a new and progressive era of system expansion based on inclusion and collaboration. However, this idea by itself, which has influenced the education profession, did not prove sufficiently politically strong to prevail in the politicised policy environment of a looming 2005 general election.

Through an understanding of how both dominant and oppositional forces develop ideas, political strategies and policies, the concept of political era can highlight the conditions for the transition between one era and another and the reasons for political failure. Reflecting upon system reform over the last two decades, it is clear that a number of factors – socio-economic, political, cultural, curricular, organisational and labour market – have to be linked together to shift a system from one equilibrium to another (Finegold and Soskice 1988; Hodgson and Spours 2003). These more general shifts may also provide conditions where political space can be afforded to radical ideas to be exchanged and adopted. The role of wider political shifts based on the convergence of a number of factors also provides a clue to current political logjams in 14–19 reform. The Tomlinson proposals for curricular change did not prevail in 2005, not only on account of government electoral pragmatism, but also because they were not explicitly linked to a broader set of changes reflected in wider social attitudes towards education. However, the Tomlinson ideas are now firmly embedded in the policy memory of many researchers, policy-makers and practitioners and, in this sense, they still serve to contest the dominant ideas of the political era in post-14 education. Arguably, therefore, both the policy process associated with the Tomlinson reform agenda and the proposals contained within the Final Report potentially provide sources of policy learning in the future when political space is opened up for more radical change. The question is whether this professional consensus can broaden its appeal. It also depends on how far the Government is able to succeed with its strategies.

Dimension 2. The education state

The second dimension of the analytical framework is the 'education state', which can be seen both as a manifestation of a political era and as a reinforcing element within it. We see the education state comprising the whole range of national, regional and local structures and institutions, including the Number 10 Policy Unit, DfES, the regulatory and awarding bodies, inspectorates, funding bodies and public and private education providers. This definition, therefore, goes beyond purely governmental institutions and quangos and tries to capture the significant role of a set of major players within the contested landscape of education policy (Ball 1990; Ozga 2000). Like Kogan (1975), we also include in our definition education pressure groups, such as professional associations, teacher unions and think tanks, as well as the education media and key individuals, all of whom exercise different degrees of political power and influence at different points in the policy process.

The education state under New Labour shows considerable continuity with the Conservative education state. It is highly centralist and uses a growing number of political advisers; it has continued to create single quangos (e.g. the QCA, the LSC and now a unified inspectorate and Quality Improvement Agency (QIA)); it continues to use arm's-length agencies and powerful steering and accountability mechanisms to drive institutional behaviour; it has increased the private/public mix in education and the role of local governance has remained weak (Hodgson et al. 2005).

There appear, however, to be two countervailing trends – devolution of power to Scotland and Wales (and possibly to the nine English regions in the longer term) and the concept of joined-up government (Cabinet Office 2000).

Reform-minded devolved governments (and this is certainly the case in terms of 14–19 education and training in Scotland and Wales) can increase pressure on England to reform and can be a source of policy learning. This is particularly the case in 14–19 education and training where significant developments are taking place in both Scotland and Wales that have similar aims to policies in England, but are different in substance and approach (see Chapters 6 and 7 in this volume).

The move to joined-up government, which relies on different government agencies working together at the local level for the good of the learner (for example through the *Every Child Matters* (DfES 2003a) agenda, may also exert a subtle pressure for reform of the education state through its reinforcement of the pivotal role for local government. Governance at the local level is important in terms of 14–19 policy and practice because it is at this level that collaboration takes place between education institutions to provide a range of learning opportunities and progression routes for learners (DfES 2005b). This type of governance and collaborative arrangement at the local level challenges both central government control and institutional autonomy. While LLSCs have struggled to introduce an element of local planning into the 14–19 education market (Hodgson *et al.* 2005), there are some powerful historical and current examples of innovative initiatives and practices in 14–19 education and training at the local level in England which take forward the unified and inclusive Tomlinson principles, despite the difficult national policy climate (Hayward *et al.* 2005).

The significance of the education state for 14–19 policy analysis is that it offers a way of understanding the interplay of different levels of governance and how space for policy-making can be afforded to the different actors within it. Discussion within the Nuffield 14–19 Review has so far concluded that a more devolved education state, representing a better balance between national, regional, local and institutional decision-making (e.g. Stanton 2004), would provide a more favourable environment not only for a more collaborative 14–19 phase, but also for the creation of a more deliberative and less mercurial or error-prone policy process which makes use of policy learning. There is a strong strand of rhetoric within government policy about seeking the right balance between national, regional and local levels of governance and promoting greater citizen empowerment (ODPM 2004; Miliband 2006b).

It is not yet clear how far the Government is prepared to go in strengthening the layer of governance at the level immediately above that of the institution because of an ideological commitment to greater provider competition (e.g. DfES 2005c). There is a distinct possibility that 'strategic partnerships' at the local level will attempt to join up initiatives and to win hearts and minds to a more collaborative agenda, but without regulatory teeth. The layer above the institution is, nevertheless, very important in terms of local policy learning in 14–19 education and training because of the space it provides for dialogue, deliberation and planning between local partners, sharing of local intelligence, translation of national policy and feeding messages back up to the regional and national levels. It is also at this level that professional memory may be able to exert some support for policy learning in terms of 'what works'. But the key issue will be one of power. The benefits of policy learning are diminished if, at the end of the day, local partners do not have the powers to enforce solutions and are not able to realise comprehensive change.

Dimension 3. The policy process

This third dimension of the analytical framework is an attempt to capture the dynamic and messy nature of policy-making from its inception to its implementation. It recognises that below the level of political and ideological intentions and within the education state, there are a complex set of actions and players that contribute to the policy process. This part of the analytical framework has to be able to accommodate and explain inequalities in the exercise of power, why crises occur, how new ideas enter the policy process and the existence of problems or opportunities with regards to policy learning.

This dimension of analysis is based upon the 'policy triangle' (Bowe *et al.* 1992), which describes three contexts within which education policy is formulated and enacted – the 'context of influence', the 'context of policy text production' and the 'context of practice'. This triangle illustrates the dynamic, contested and cyclical nature of the policy process and the role of key players within it. Practitioners are seen as contributors to the policy process and there is a recognition that policy is not simply a transmission-belt from central government downwards. The model thus helps to explain why policies may be conceived in one way at the level of policy text production, for example, but be interpreted in another at the level of practice, and how both intended and unintended outcomes may occur. It also helps to explain how different parties in the policy-making process might have a privileged position at different points in the policy cycle. Practitioners, for example, are likely to have little power at the point where policies are conceived, but the balance of power may move strongly in their favour at the point where the policy is enacted and where they can either mould or subvert government intentions. Each corner of the policy triangle, but particularly the context of practice, offers potential for policy learning in 14–19 education and training, which we illustrate by using the model to briefly narrate recent 14–19 events.

Context of influence

Ideas for a unified 14–19 curriculum and qualifications system had been building gradually during the 1990s and eventually broke surface in terms of official policy discussion through the Government's response to the 14–19 Green Paper (DfES 2003b). However, there was a split within the highest levels of government about how far to take curriculum and qualifications reform. Some ministers, David Miliband in particular, wanted a unified solution and took advantage of the 2002 A-level crisis to advocate this radical path. Others, even closer to the Prime Minister, kept a low profile during the deliberations of the Tomlinson Working Group and used the context of a looming general election to impose a more divided solution. Policy minds now appear closed as government commits itself to implementation of the 14–19 White Paper. However, if there are problems with implementation, as we think is inevitable, a host of national bodies and sections of the media will be eager to remind the Government that it did have another strategic option.

Context of text production

While the 14–19 White Paper and *The 14–19 Implementation Plan* are the dominant texts, the Tomlinson Final Report remains as an alternative text and a source of policy learning. Wiped from the DfES website, this text and responses from the profession and beyond can be found lodged on various sites across the Internet (e.g. http://education.guardian.co.uk/1419education). A key issue is whether there will be a re-run of the debate that took place around the production of the Tomlinson Report in the proposed 2008 curriculum and qualifications review.

Context of practice

The Government is dependent on schools, colleges, work-based learning providers, local authorities and LLSCs to implement 14–19 reform. It is at this level that there is real potential for policy learning because there is a greater sense of openness – each of the parties has something to contribute, based on experience, and each has the need to learn. There is also an explicit acknowledgement by government that mutual learning should take place at the local level (DfES 2005b and Chapter 3 in this volume).

The ability to learn and to be able to respond effectively to learning from experience will be, however, affected by structural barriers. Radical ideas about strong area-wide measures to strengthen institutional collaboration at the local level could be thwarted by policy levers and drivers that incentivise institutional competition, while progressive ideas to develop more integrated learning programmes for all 14–19 year olds will mean challenging existing and new qualifications divisions. Effective policy learning, therefore, will require not only a recognition of what has worked at a local level, but also of what has not been allowed to work and why.

Dimension 4. Political space

The concept of 'political space' describes the opening up of opportunity for different stakeholders to influence the policy process. Political space can be realised in several ways – it can be created by the 'battle of ideas' over a period of time; it can result from spaces afforded in the reform process either intentionally (for example, by encouraging bottom-up practitioner developments or from more open forms of consultation) or unintentionally (as the result of crises). Political space can also be reinforced by what we term 'tipping debates'.[1]

Researchers and practitioners can both create political space and work within it. As we have seen, in the case of 14–19 curriculum and qualifications reform in England, researchers, professional associations and think tanks worked together for more than a decade to create a 'tipping debate' about the development of a flexible and unified 14-plus curriculum and qualifications system. This long-term work, combined with the effects of the A-level crisis, created the political space for researchers and practitioners to work 'for policy' within the Tomlinson 14–19 Working Group and the professional and political groups aligned with it. However, these same groups were not party to the deliberations on the proposals within the subsequent 14–19 White Paper, which was drafted by civil servants and political advisers.

Political space can, therefore, be opened up and closed down by government at any stage in the policy process. The 14–19 White Paper, with its political compromises, serves to remind the researcher and practitioner communities of the temporary nature of political space made recently available within the English system. These 'closed/contested' or at the very least 'unstable/fluctuating' approaches to political space at the national level in England can be contrasted to policy-making in Wales. Here, considerable effort has been made by the Assembly Government to afford spaces to different groups through, for example, the establishment of a range of 'task and finish groups' as part of the development of the *Learning Pathways 14–19* reforms (WAG 2002; 2006). There is a widespread recognition that policy-making in Wales is more open and consultative than in England (e.g. Daugherty *et al.* 2000; Rees 2003) with a greater willingness to engage in evidence-based policy-making, although there are problems with the ability of a relatively small policy-maker community to properly utilise research evidence (see Chapter 1 in this volume). It is our contention that providing more political space for researchers and practitioners to work alongside policy-makers in a more shared policy-making process also opens up the door to more effective policy learning.

A more collective and deliberative policy process for effective policy learning

The principal reason for developing the four-dimensional framework for analysing 14–19 education policy is to enable researchers, practitioners and policy-makers themselves to assess when and how to engage in the policy process in order to bring about improvements to the education system and to the policy process itself.

Different points in the policy process offer varying balances of constraints and opportunities for intervention and contribution by different parties, from the most critical to the most practical. These may include challenging orthodoxies, creating political space, developing system thinking, working with policy memory, pointing out possible unintended policy outcomes, stimulating policy learning, developing strategy and undertaking evaluation to aid improvement. The issue is knowing when and how to act in the best interests of learners, teachers and wider society.

The framework suggests the need to move toward what Hajer and Wagenaar (2003) term a more 'deliberative' approach to policy-making, which would improve the climate of policy-making and the opportunities for policy learning. First, it recognises the importance of a more collective historical sense of post-14 education and training across the different communities and a shared appreciation of past successes and failures. Presently, there is a profoundly ahistorical approach to policy-making (Hencke and Leigh 2006), which serves to deny policy memory and valuable professional and researcher experience. Second, the framework argues for an opening up of the education state to create the structures and levels of decision-making for more participative policy-making and for policy learning at the local level. Third, and linked to this, is the need for a less politicised policy process, conducted at a slower pace than at present to provide space for policy learning and to produce a greater degree of consensus through dialogue. Fourth, the framework argues that we have to move from 'contested' to 'afforded' political space in which all three communities (policy-makers, practitioners and researchers) have a place at all points in the policy process and not just at the point of implementation when the big decisions have been made on narrow political grounds.

Acknowledgement

The authors would like to acknowledge that material for this chapter draws substantially on an article by them in the *Journal of Education Policy*, (21) 6: 'An analytical framework for policy engagement: the contested case of 14–19 reform in England'.

Note

1. The term 'tipping debates' is a reworking of 'tipping point', a concept popularised by Malcolm Gladwell (2002) to explain how ideas, products, messages and behaviours, facilitated by key types of communicators, can cross a threshold and achieve a critical mass. Tipping debates refer to areas of ideological contestation where fundamental debates (e.g. in the case of 14–19 education – on curriculum and qualifications, learning, skills, achievement and so on) can be tipped in different directions to gain professional and popular support.

References

Ball, S.J. (1990) *Politics and Policy-making in Education: Explorations in policy sociology*. London: Routledge.

— (1997) 'Sociology and critical research: a personal review of recent education policy and policy research'. *British Education Research Journal*, 23 (3), 257–74.

Bowe, R., Ball, S.J. and Gold, A. (1992) *Reforming Education and Changing Schools: Case-studies in policy sociology*. London: Routledge.

Cabinet Office (2000) *Wiring It Up: Whitehall's management of cross-cutting policies and services*. London: Cabinet Office.

Clarke, J. and Newman, J. (2004) 'Governing in the modern world?' In L. Steinberg, and R. Johnson (eds), *Blairism and the War of Persuasion*. London: Lawrence and Wishart.

Clarke, J., Gewirtz, S. and McLaughlin, E. (eds) (2000) *New Managerialism, New Welfare?* London: Sage and Open University Press.

Daugherty, R., Phillips, R. and Rees, G. (2000) 'Education policy-making and devolved governance in Wales: past, present and future'. In R. Daugherty, R. Phillips and G. Rees (eds), *Education Policy-Making in Wales: Explorations in devolved governance*. Cardiff: University of Wales Press.

Department for Education and Skills (DfES) (2002) *14–19 Education: Extending opportunities, raising standards*. London: DfES.

— (2003a) *Every Child Matters*. London: DfES.

— (2003b) *14–19: Opportunity and Excellence; government response to the 14–19 Green Paper*. London: DfES.

— (2005a) *14–19 Education and Skills*. London: DfES.

— (2005b) *The 14–19 Implementation Plan*. London: DfES.

— (2005c) *Higher Standards, Better Schools for All: More choice for parents and pupils*. London: DfES.

Du Gay, P. (2000) 'Entrepreneurial governance and public management: the anti-bureaucrats'. In J. Clarke, S. Gerwitz and E. McLaughlin. (eds), *New Managerialism, New Welfare?* London: Sage and Open University Press.

Finegold, D. and Soskice, D. (1988) 'The failure of training in Britain: analysis and prescription', *Oxford Review of Economic Policy*, 4 (3), 21–53.

Finegold, D., Keep, E., Miliband, D., Raffe, D., Spours, K. and Young, M. (1990) *A British Baccalaureate: Overcoming divisions between education and training*. London: Institute of Public Policy Research (IPPR).

Gladwell, M. (2002) *How Little Things Can Make a Big Difference*. Boston: Bay Back Books.

Hajer, M. and Wagenaar, H. (2003) *Deliberative Policy Analysis: Understanding governance in the network society*. Cambridge: Cambridge University Press.

Hayward, G., Hodgson, A., Johnson, J., Oancea, A., Pring, R., Spours, K., Wright, S. and Wilde, S. (2005) *Annual Report of the Nuffield 14–19 Review 2004–5*. OUDES: University of Oxford.

Hencke, D. and Leigh, D. (2006) 'Blair lacks sense of ethical priorities, says anti-sleaze watchdog'. *Guardian*, 28 April.

Higham, J. and Yeomans, D. (2005) 'Policy memory and policy amnesia in 14–19 education: learning from the past?' Discussion Paper 5, Seminar on Policy Learning in 14–19 Education, 15 March. Online. Available HTTP: www.nuffield14–19review.org.uk/documents.shtml (accessed 17 September 2006).

Higham, J., Sharp, P. and Yeomans, D. (2002) *Changing the 14–19 School Curriculum in England: Lessons from successive reforms*. Research Report to the Economic and Social Research Council. Swindon: Economic and Social Research Council (ESRC).

Hodgson, A. and Spours, K. (2003) *Beyond A Levels: Curriculum 2000 and the reform of 14–19 qualifications.* London: Kogan Page.

Hodgson, A. and Spours, K. (2004) 'Reforming 14–19 learning: towards a new comprehensive phase of education'. *New Economy,* 11 (4), 217–23.

Hodgson, A., Spours, K., Coffield, F., Steer, R., Finlay. I., Edward, S. and Gregson, M. (2005) *A New Learning and Skills Landscape? The LSC within the learning and skills sector.* Research Report 1, TLRP project 'Learning and inclusion within the new Learning and Skills Sector'. Institute of Education, University of London.

Kogan, M. (1975) *Educational Policymaking: A study of interest groups in Parliament.* London: George Allen and Unwin.

Lasonen, J. and Young, M. (eds) (1998) *Strategies for Achieving Parity of Esteem in European Upper Secondary Education.* Jyväskylä: Institute for Educational Research, University of Jyväskylä.

Local Government Association (LGA) (2004) *Local Government – Transforming learning, building skills in education, in communities, at work: LGA position statement.* London: LGA.

Miliband, D. Rt. Hon. (2006a) 'Empowerment and the deal for devolution'. Speech to the annual conference of the New Local Government Network, 18 January.

— (2006b) 'Empowerment and respect: building change from the bottom up'. Speech at the Cleaner, Safer, Greener Conference, 'A Vision of Respect', 13 March.

Newman, J. (2000) 'Beyond the new public management? Modernising public services'. In J. Clarke, S. Gerwitz and E. McLaughlin. (eds), *New Managerialism, New Welfare?* London: Sage and Open University Press.

Office of the Deputy Prime Minister (ODPM) (2004) *The Future of Local Government: Developing a 10 year vision.* London: Local Government Strategy Unit.

Ozga, J. (2000) *Policy Research in Education Settings: Contested terrain.* Buckingham: Open University Press.

Phillips, R. and Furlong, J. (2001) *Education, Reform and the State: Twenty-five years of politics, policy and practice.* London: RoutledgeFalmer.

Raffe, D. (2005) 'Learning from "home international" comparisons: 14–19 curriculum and qualifications reform in England, Scotland and Wales'. Discussion Paper 3 presented at a joint seminar of Education and Youth Transitions Project and the Nuffield Review, 15 March. Online. Available HTTP:

www.nuffield14–19review.org.uk/documents.shtml (accessed 17 September 2006).

Rees, G. (2003) *Democratic Devolution and Education Policy in Wales: The emergence of a national system?* Cardiff: Cardiff School of Social Sciences, Cardiff University.

Stanton, G. (2004) 'The organisation of full-time 14–19 provision in the state sector'. Paper presented to Nuffield 14–19 Review, Working Day 3, 1 April 2004. Online. Available HTTP:www.nuffield14–19review.org.uk/documents.shtml (accessed 17 September 2006).

Steinberg, L. and Johnson, R. (eds) (2004) 'Introduction'. In L. Steinberg and R. Johnson (eds), *Blairism and the War of Persuasion*. London: Lawrence and Wishart.

Welsh Assembly Government (WAG) (2002) *Learning Pathways 14–19: Consultation document*. Cardiff: WAG.

— (2006) *Learning Pathways 14–19 Action Plan*. Cardiff: WAG.

Working Group on 14–19 Reform (2004) *14–19 Curriculum and Qualifications Reform: Final report*. London: DfES.

9 Policy learning in 14–19 education: from accusation to an agenda for improvement

David Raffe and Ken Spours

Risky assumptions about policy learning in the 14–19 context

This book started with two assumptions about the potential for policy learning in 14–19 education and training. The first concerned the possibility of learning from previous experience. In England and Wales, many current issues in 14–19 education and training have been on the agenda at least since the dramatic changes to patterns of full-time participation in the mid-1980s. A similar situation pertains in Scotland, where the 1980s saw the introduction of the first unified curriculum and qualifications framework for all 14–16 year olds and the 16-plus *Action Plan* which prefigured a more flexible and unified curriculum beyond 16. In the two decades that have followed there has been ample opportunity for policy-makers to learn from these earlier developments and debates in post-14 education when making policy decisions on such issues as the curriculum, institutional arrangements and labour-market environment needed to expand participation and improve achievement. The second of our assumptions concerned opportunities to learn from cross-national comparisons and, in particular, from 'home international' comparison of policy developments in the home countries of Great Britain. England, Scotland and Wales, in their own ways, have continued to develop distinctive policies and policy processes. At the same time, all three systems share certain UK-wide characteristics, and within this nexus of similarity and distinctiveness lie opportunities for mutual learning. A third assumption emerged as we researched the book. This is that governments have wished to engage in policy learning as part of modern approaches to governance such as evidence-based policy-making, policies based on 'what works' and joined-up government. This raises the questions of whether, and how, these approaches have been pursued in practice and what kinds of policy learning have resulted.

An important question, of course, is the kind of learning that policy-makers are prepared or able to undertake. Policy-makers in England, in the period 1998 to 2003, were interested primarily in learning across policy departments and informing policy with research, motivated by a 'joined-up government' agenda. Over the last year or so, and in relation to the *14–19 Implementation Plan* (DfES 2005), the Government's focus has been more on delivery and implementation of its 14–19 reforms, reflecting an interest in the exchange of good/best practice.

Policy-makers in Scotland and Wales have sought to learn from the views and experiences of practitioners and stakeholders. In Scotland they have engaged practitioners in the development and diffusion of innovations in assessment and curriculum. In Wales they have attempted to be inclusive through the involvement of a range of stakeholders in 'Task and Finish Groups'.

What governments say they want to do and what they actually end up doing may, of course, be different because of wider political pressures. A broadly shared assumption, which runs through several chapters, is that policy-making is affected by the wider political environment. Greater levels of social consensus within a political system or, at least, political interdependence through coalition, may provide a more open political environment for policy-making and therefore, for policy learning. However, as the experiences of Scotland and Wales illustrate, the strength of this consensus may come to have more influence on policy-making than the strength of the available evidence. And as the devolved administrations become increasingly committed to specific policy directions they may find it uncomfortable to maintain an open political environment in which the chosen policy directions can more easily be challenged. On the other hand, more contested environments may result in higher levels of 'politicisation' of policy-making, as found in England, which can dominate or defect the best of intentions in policy-making and policy learning. Differences in the wider political climate in the three home international countries thus raise different possibilities and problems for policy learning, and provide some explanation for the varied patterns of policy learning in England, Scotland and Wales.

In the case of England, the development of the 14–19 phase has proved highly contentious with major strategic disagreement over the 14–19 White Paper's rejection of the main proposals of the Tomlinson Report. The main points of disagreement between the government and the practitioner and research communities include the extent to which GCSEs and A levels should be reformed alongside vocational qualifications and the role of institutional competition. In the case of Scotland and Wales the picture is rather different. While there are disagreements within Scotland over curriculum flexibility and the further reform of National Qualifications, and within Wales over the implementation of *14–19 Learning Pathways* and the Welsh Baccalaureate, the broad goals of policy are not contested to the same extent as in England. This stronger strategic consensus in Scotland and Wales is partly a result of not following the same agenda as in England. Strategic agreement does not automatically guarantee a climate for policy learning but, as we shall see, it does appear to help.

We have assumed, therefore, that policy-makers wish to engage in a learning process but the question is what kind of learning takes place. Learning can be narrow and fleeting or more expansive and continual. By focusing, in the first instance, on learning from the past and from home international comparisons, we may have set the learning bar quite high.

Moreover, and especially at the present political juncture, we may have exposed ourselves to three possible criticisms. The first is the charge of *naïvety* and *unrealistic expectations*: that when we pose questions about policy learning we implicitly expect policy-makers to act rationally in pursuit of the public interest. The second is the charge of *policy disappointment* or *sour grapes*: that some of us are motivated by our own disappointment and frustration arising from the Government's rejection of the Tomlinson proposals, of which we were co-authors, and that like parents with wayward children we blame the Government's behaviour on its inability to learn. The third is the charge of *negativity*: that we are quick to attack an easy target in our criticisms of recent policy-making, but slow to move beyond critique and to develop constructive proposals for improving policy learning.

In the rest of this final chapter we review the contributions to the book in the light of these three charges. To address the charge of naïvety and unrealistic expectations we re-examine the concept(s) of policy learning outlined in the various chapters and ask whether they constitute a reasonable and defensible way of evaluating policy-making and policy learning. To address the charge of sour grapes resulting from policy disappointment, we review the evidence offered in these chapters that there have indeed been failures of policy learning in 14–19 education in England, Scotland and Wales, not only in relation to learning historically and comparatively but also in relation to other learning goals that governments have set themselves, such as learning from local innovation. And to address the charge of negativity we review the explanations for such failures offered by the different chapters, and consider whether they point towards an agenda for improvement.

Naïvety and unrealistic expectations?

We first address the charge of naïvety: does our concept of policy learning make unrealistic assumptions about how policy is made or about how it could be expected to be made? A clear conclusion of this book is that while there may be areas of agreement (e.g. that policy learning is an essentially shared activity and is desirable) there is no single, agreed concept of policy learning itself. Despite their overlapping authorship, the chapters exemplify differing concepts and understandings of policy learning. They approach the policy learner, sources of policy learning, policy knowledge and the policy learning process from a range of perspectives.

The policy learner(s)

A majority of chapters view policy learning as something that is engaged in primarily by governments and public authorities (e.g. Higham and Yeomans; Hart and Tuck; Stasz and Wright). In some chapters policy learning is seen as more widely dispersed around policy communities and systems of governance (e.g. Raffe and Spours; Spours, Hodgson and Yeomans). In the latter view, practitioners and researchers are also important, indeed essential, participants in policy learning because of the role they can play both in the formulation of policy and in its implementation. In varying degrees, all these chapters share a view of policy learning as a collective activity that is not simply reducible to the individual learning experiences of policy-makers. An alternative perspective, outlined by Lumby and Foskett, argues that learning must be understood as a distinct activity of individual policy-makers, whose goals and motivations may differ from those of other potential policy contributors. This perspective complements the other views expressed in this book by warning us that, even if policy-making is a shared process, different parties will not share identical interests.

Sources of learning

Some chapters focus on learning from the experience of earlier policies: for example, Higham and Yeomans' discussion of policy memory and policy amnesia in England, and Hart and Tuck's account of successive curriculum and qualifications reforms in Scotland. Other chapters, including those by Raffe and by Stasz and Wright, discuss learning from other countries, especially the other countries of the UK. However, the general thrust of all contributions points to policy learning based on a wide range of resources and contexts. Most authors acknowledge that policy development continues during implementation, reflecting a broad and cyclical concept of the policy process that embraces learning from the current experience of practitioners and others who are trialling or implementing policy. Several authors consider that this overlap of policy development and implementation promotes policy learning because it provides for earlier and fuller feedback on the current policy (Spours, Hodgson and Yeomans; Hodgson and Spours). However, Hart and Tuck, reflecting on the evolutionary Scottish experience over a 20-year period, see overlaps of policy development and implementation as an obstacle to learning from history because new policies cannot always be based on systematic analysis and evaluation of earlier experiences.

The nature of policy knowledge

Most authors appear to share Raffe's view that policy learning is considerably broader than policy borrowing and that the knowledge that results is much more than the mere identification of policies that work or of best practice. Several authors, including Lumby and Foskett and Raffe, distinguish between single-loop learning that corrects implementation and more radical double-loop learning that challenges policy assumptions. Spours, Hodgson and Yeomans, in their analysis of 14–19 Pathfinders, apply these concepts respectively to learning that is focused on practice and to learning that focuses on policy parameters, such as the targets, funding levers and other arm's-length mechanisms of the 'top-down performance management' which has become the preferred mode of governance in the English learning and skills sector. They introduce the concept of 'half-loop' learning, to express the constraints on single-loop learning that result from rigid policy agendas and rushed policy processes.

The learning process

The chapters express different views about rational models of policy-making. On the one hand, several authors attribute failures of policy learning to gaps in information and barriers to rational policy-making (e.g. Higham and Yeomans; Hart and Tuck; Stasz and Wright); we discuss these barriers in more detail below. On the other hand, Raffe and Spours argue that the rationalist model of policy-making is itself flawed. Policy learning is unlikely to be optimal in such a model, which is procedural and potentially insular because of its focus on policy-making processes within the policy community itself. It may not, therefore, ascribe a sufficiently active role to the practitioner or the independent researcher in what has become a much more complex world of reform. Lumby and Foskett also argue that a rationalist model of policy-making may have perverse consequences. Rational behaviour may involve 'gaming' in which stakeholders seek to maximise their individual gains, and rational argument may encourage defensive responses which make it harder to correct defective policies.

A related issue concerns the relationship between political conflict and policy learning. On the one hand, most authors reject a technocratic view in which political factors prevent or distort sound decision-making based on policy learning. This rejection is expressed most explicitly by Higham and Yeomans and by Raffe and Spours who, in their collaborative model, note that political contestation may complement and promote policy learning. On the other hand, several authors describe tensions between policy learning and political factors (e.g. Raffe and Spours; Hart and Tuck; Raffe; Hodgson and Spours). Political and ideological conditions define the context for policy learning and influence the extent and nature of learning that occurs (e.g. Higham and Yeomans; Hodgson and Spours). For example, Hart and Tuck point out that both in Scotland and in England reforms have been constrained by governments' refusal to countenance the abolition of 'gold standard' academic qualifications.

Connecting policy learning, policy-making and the policy process

Running through the chapters are two distinct but related discourses of policy learning and of the relation between policy learning and effective policy-making. Several chapters move between the two discourses.

The first discourse assumes that policy learning increases the effectiveness of policies in the pursuit of goals that are consensual or, at least, legitimated through democratic political processes. Learning occurs when policies incorporate lessons that can be drawn from the evidence that is available, or potentially available, to policy-makers. This 'normative' discourse typically uses social-scientific modes of analysis to debate the reasonableness of policies in the light of this evidence. It focuses on the logical and methodological connections between the evidence and the policy outcomes, not on the policy processes through which these connections were – or were not – made.

Several chapters in the book offer methodological advice to support this kind of social-scientific learning. Raffe advocates 'home international' comparisons as a source of learning, and discusses the types of learning that they can support. Stasz and Wright present a policy instruments and institutions framework as a conceptual tool for policy learning. Hart and Tuck discuss the transferability of learning across different policy contexts or across different policy strategies. A fourth chapter, by Hodgson and Spours, advocates a framework of conceptual tools – political eras, education state, policy process and political space – to be used by different contributors to policy-making in order to create a shared historical and systemic understanding of 14–19 policy; however, their framework relates to policy processes as well as the analysis of policy itself, and therefore straddles the two discourses. Other chapters within the first (normative) discourse apply this type of social-scientific reasoning to actual policies, and ask to what extent they are consistent with the evidence on which the policy-makers could draw. Thus, Higham and Yeomans examine three recent curriculum and qualifications policies in England and ask to what extent they incorporate the lessons of earlier policy experiences. Stasz and Wright similarly apply their framework to current vocational education policies across the UK in order to identify apparent weaknesses such as the neglect of capacity-building policy instruments. Lumby and Foskett review policies in English 14–19 education over the past quarter-century, and note that they have generated considerable 'turbulence' but little substantive change. Spours, Hodgson and Yeomans point to the inconsistency between the policy levers and drivers employed by central government and the evidence from local experiments that these levers and drivers constrain innovation.

The second discourse of policy learning is concerned with the policy process: with the structures and mechanisms of policy-making and governance and the extent and nature of the learning processes that occur within them. We introduced this discourse in Chapter 1 in our discussion of rationalist, collaborative and politicised models of policy-making and policy learning, and in our attempts to apply these models to England, Scotland and Wales. This wider context of policy learning affects the motivation of policy-makers to learn, what to learn and whom to include in the learning process. Several other chapters (e.g. Higham and Yeomans; Spours, Hodgson and Yeomans; Lumby and Foskett; Raffe; Hodgson and Spours) explore the relationship between the policy process and policy learning in order to explain why actual experience fails to live up to the expectations of the normative concept. Lumby and Foskett put it succinctly when they remark 'policy learning does take place but as learning of a particular character'.

Different levels of expectation

This brings us back to the question of naïvety. Is it naïve to pose questions in terms of the normative discourse of policy learning: to ask if policies are consistent with the evidence from earlier policy experiences, from other countries or from local trialling and implementation? At one level, clearly not, because policy-makers expect this of themselves and there is evidence from Cabinet Office sources that they have deliberated this issue. However, it may be naïve to pose questions in terms of the normative discourse of policy learning without recognising that the answers or their explanations may lie in the second discourse, that is, in the policy process. The issue of debate lies in the relationship between the two discourses: how can the policy process be developed to facilitate learning to a high standard of the normative model? Some chapters caution judgement by recognising the challenges of policy-making and policy learning from the perspective of the policy-maker and the day-to-day political and capacity pressures they face. In this sense, we recognise that there is a gap between the expectations of the normative model and the realities of the policy process. But in the end, the expectations stand because we believe that the 'reason-ability' of policies, and their compatibility with available evidence and experience, are appropriate criteria by which they should be judged.

We therefore disagree with Olsen and Peters' (1996) argument, which we cited in Chapter 1, that it is wrong to apply the norms, procedures and criteria of social science (our first discourse) to political decision-making (the second). We believe that it is appropriate to generate expectations in terms of a social-science perspective, but these should be tempered by a notion of what is realistic in terms of the policy process. In their different ways, the chapters start to assemble reasonable, sympathetic but also ambitious sets of expectations regarding policy learning in the current policy context.

Expectations about policy learning are generated in different contexts and, ultimately, their reasonability has to be judged within these. Expectations or assumptions could be considered on a sliding scale, from the less to the more ambitious. First, we expect policy-makers to accept that policies can and should be judged against the lessons of history, of international comparisons and of local experimentation. That is, we expect them to recognise the legitimacy of the normative discourse, while accepting also that democratic politics provides a different and sometimes conflicting basis for legitimacy. Second, we expect policy-makers to acknowledge the diversity of forms of policy learning and policy knowledge, including the value of double-loop learning. This is a more ambitious expectation because it potentially involves a change in policy-making styles. So does the third expectation, which is that policy-makers actively search for and collect the historical, comparative and local evidence required for policy learning, and use it to inform policy decisions. Finally, and most ambitious of all, we expect the policy process itself to be organised in a way that supports an effective, deliberative and inclusive model of policy learning. We explore how this can be done later in the chapter.

Disappointment and sour grapes? Evidence for the failure of policy learning

Having argued that we are not naïve – or perhaps that the naïvety of our expectations is both desirable and necessary – we now address the second charge, of sour grapes. We cannot claim to be neutral observers of 14–19 policy. A sceptical reader might suspect that our dissatisfaction with the policy process in England reflects the relative failure of our ideas to influence policy there; conversely, our relative satisfaction with policy processes in Scotland may reflect its greater receptiveness – so far – to our arguments. It is perhaps natural that academics should believe that governments that accept their advice are good learners, and vice versa. So is there any stronger evidence of learning failure and, more precisely, of the failure of policy processes to meet the expectations of the normative concept of policy learning?

The chapters in this book provide two types of evidence for this failure, broadly corresponding to the two discourses outlined above. The first, closer to the normative discourse, is based on the outputs or outcomes of the policy process itself. In our opening chapter we presented the 'case for the prosecution' by pointing to areas of policy, in Scotland and Wales as well as in England, where policy-makers appear to have ignored the lessons of earlier policies and experience elsewhere. This realisation has resulted in dissatisfaction with the outcomes of the policy process among practitioners and stakeholders in 14–19 education. Higham and Yeomans explore this theme in more detail; they show how current English policies in three areas – flexibility in the 14–16 curriculum, vocational diplomas and employer engagement – fail to address key issues raised by the experience of related policies and debates over the past 25 years. Higham and Yeomans cannot directly observe the processes that led to this failure; their analysis is based largely on their analysis of the outcomes of these processes. Stasz and Wright similarly point to false assumptions that underlie recent policies for vocational education. They suggest that the choice of policy instruments by the home governments – in particular their relative neglect of capacity-building instruments – reflects a failure of policy learning. Lumby and Foskett refer to policy outcomes in a broader sense when they argue that policies have failed to change the system's underlying principles or its ultimate outputs. The chapters by Hart and Tuck and by Raffe also identify policy lessons that might have been learnt but which were not reflected in actual policy.

This evidence is reinforced by the perceptions of policy-makers themselves. Hart and Tuck, in a chapter which draws extensively on the accounts of other policy-makers as well as their own participation in the processes they describe, refer to a range of factors which were perceived to limit the transferability of lessons from other policy contexts. Raffe notes that few policy-makers interviewed in the 1990s and 2000s believed that home international comparisons had had much influence on policy. And policy-makers' silence can be eloquent: Higham and Yeomans note that the issues raised by earlier policy experiences are neither acknowledged nor addressed in public policy documents and justifications for the three policies they analyse. Spours, Hodgson and Yeomans note that policy-makers' own reflections on local innovation tend to be used as forms of policy legitimation in policy documents rather than as a source of policy analysis.

The second type of evidence, closer to the second discourse, refers to the actual processes of policy-making, and to the numerous factors that have inhibited the flow of information, the learning process or the links between learning and policy development. Nearly all the chapters identify, or at least speculate about, barriers to policy learning arising from the nature of the policy process as well as the complexity of the 14–19 field itself. However, identifying these barriers is the first step to removing them. We therefore save our review of this evidence for the next and final section of this chapter, in which we address the charge of 'negativity' and consider how to improve policy learning.

Negativity? How to improve policy learning

The chapters in this book provide evidence that there have indeed been failures of policy learning – as judged against the normative concept – in 14–19 education in Britain in recent years. It is possible, indeed likely, that such failures are also characteristic of policy in other fields, in other countries and at other times. This book did not set out to address these broader comparative and historical issues. Nevertheless it provides evidence that failures of policy learning are not a constant and, by implication, unalterable feature of all policy-making. Policy learning is variable. It is – at least at present – more effective in Scotland and Wales than in England (Raffe and Spours). It is more evident in some policy decisions than in others (Hart and Tuck). It is shaped by wider political and ideological conditions, by institutional structures and more broadly by the system of governance (Higham and Yeomans; Spours, Hodgson and Yeomans; Hart and Tuck; Hodgson and Spours). Examining these influences on policy learning may give us clues on how to improve it. The chapters in the book identify four main barriers to policy learning, and consequently four main areas for improvement.

Data and methodological issues in policy learning

Several chapters (Hart and Tuck; Raffe; Stasz and Wright; Hodgson and Spours) draw attention to barriers to policy learning associated with the limited knowledge base and the methodology of policy learning. Even when governments try diligently to learn from earlier experience or from other countries, the lessons may be very difficult to draw. The experience from which to learn may be too scarce, or too narrow, or too context-bound. Lessons may not transfer easily between countries or between policy environments or political eras. They may not transfer easily between types of policy: for example, between policies which address particular sectors of education and 'unifying' or comprehensive policies which embrace all sectors (Hart and Tuck). Such problems are familiar to social scientists, who have discussed at length the limits and possibilities of (for example) policy learning from cross-national comparisons.

We cannot pretend that these barriers are easy or simple to overcome, but we can suggest three steps that would help. The first is to enhance the knowledge base for policy learning. The ESRC project on Education and Youth Transitions, one of the projects which has supported the preparation of this book, has drawn attention to the weakness of the youth cohort surveys – one of the main data series for 14–19 education – as a source of evidence either on trends over time or on comparisons across parts of Great Britain (Croxford 2006). There are many other limitations if not complete gaps in the data record. Recent governments have acknowledged the need for better data, and have made considerable efforts to improve the situation. However, a change in mindset may also be needed. For example, the DfES has acknowledged the limitations of youth cohort study data as a source of trends, but it has defended this situation on the grounds that the surveys' main function is to monitor and inform current policy, not to measure trends. This response betrays a misunderstanding of the demands of policy learning, which requires rigorous trend data in order to map the historical context of current policy-making and to evaluate the impact of earlier policies.

This points to a second step, which is for members of policy communities to develop more sophisticated understandings of the methodologies of policy learning. This not only involves acquiring better knowledge on techniques of policy evaluation or appraisal; it also involves recognising the diversity of types of policy knowledge and of modes of policy learning. The issues in transferring policy lessons, described above, are less of an obstacle to some of the broader purposes of policy learning such as those outlined in the chapter by Raffe. At present, these broader purposes are not widely recognised. Learning from other countries, to take one example, will remain at a primitive level for as long as policy-makers understand this to be primarily about identifying effective policies and practices which can be introduced at home.

The third step is to develop ways to learn more effectively from local innovation and policy experimentation. The English system, in particular, has a rich tradition of local innovation which is, at present, poorly utilised for policy learning. The programmes which aim to harness this source of learning need to be re-designed so that they genuinely contribute to policy learning rather than to policy legitimation. This, too, requires a change in mindset. The governments which plan these programmes need to encourage them to engage in the kind of double-loop learning which includes the governments' own policies and control mechanisms as topics for examination. And effective learning from local innovation requires much longer timescales for policy development.

Designing institutions for policy learning

The second area for improvement relates to institutional change. There is scope to increase institutions' potential for policy learning by enhancing their research and reflective capacities. To give the Government credit, extensive work has been done through the Cabinet Office in this area, but it does not seem as prominent now as in the recent past. The challenges of increasing capacity are particularly acute in the devolved administrations, especially Wales where the increased demands of devolved government placed heavy burdens on a small civil service.

However, there are further ways in which institutions can be designed to encourage policy learning. Lumby and Foskett suggest that institutions can shape the calculation of gain and loss for individual policy-makers, and thus increase their willingness to apply policy learning in the collective interest. They also note that policy-makers in stable institutional structures have more time to understand the 'game strategies' of other players, making it more likely that individual decisions will be co-ordinated for the public good. Institutions need a level of stability if they are to develop a culture of policy learning, accumulate historical awareness and policy memory, identify and assemble relevant evidence and deliberate on the policy implications. This greater stability embraces institutional continuity, structural stability within institutions and lower turnover of staffing. Policy memory is unlikely to accumulate in institutions which are frequently restructured, or whose staff are too mobile (Higham and Yeomans; Raffe and Spours).

Political institutions can encourage shorter or longer timescales.

Stasz and Wright contrast the conveyor belt of ministers in the English DfES with the longevity of ministers in Wales. But even in Scotland, as Hart and Tuck note, demands for speedy policy-making make effective policy learning more difficult.

Strong local structures above the level of the school or college are necessary if local knowledge is to be shared among practitioners as well as fed back to government in an effective way. Policy learning can be stimulated by a robust layer of local government or equivalent institutions, as well as by collaborative partnerships of local institutions. However, Stasz and Wright observe that effective collaboration does not just happen, but requires time and resources. Collaborative partnerships need stability and long-term horizons if they are to forge the relationships of mutual understanding and trust necessary for them to become effective sites of learning. Spours, Hodgson and Yeomans note that 14–19 partnerships have to 'mature' and be developed in order to be able to learn from the experience of others and to be able to feed back into the policy process.

Finally, existing institutional links between the UK governments could be redrawn, in order better to exploit their potential to support policy learning and exchange. Raffe notes that governmental relationships between the UK's home countries rarely function in a way to promote mutual learning; similar arguments probably apply to inter-governmental links at European and global levels.

Ideological and cultural conditions for policy learning

The third area for improvement is to develop a culture of policy learning within policy communities. We have mentioned some aspects of this already: for example, the need for policy-makers to recognise that policy learning is broader than policy borrowing or the search for best practice; and the need for a changed mindset to underpin the collection of data for policy analysis. A policy-making culture which promotes evidence-informed policy is to be encouraged, but it will depend not only on the capacities of policy-makers to handle evidence but on a number of more radical shifts.

First, several chapters (e.g. Higham and Yeomans; Hodgson and Spours) point to the ahistorical nature of much policy-making and argue that policy communities need to develop a greater historical awareness. The current lack of historical understanding is reflected in the DfES's attitude to youth cohort study data, mentioned above. Higham and Yeomans describe 'a policy discourse in which the emphasis is upon the new, the radical, the innovative', which tends to deny that the past has much relevance to future policy-making. The policy culture needs to recognise that radical innovations can only succeed if they are grounded in knowledge of the past and an understanding of how to break free of its constraints.

Second, greater historical awareness, together with awareness of other systems, can encourage a deeper questioning approach or what has been termed double-loop learning. At present, policy learning tends to take place within narrow political or ideological parameters. Hodgson and Spours note that policy learning is often bounded by political eras and the ideologies that define them. Hart and Tuck describe the problems of learning across changing political contexts, and Raffe observes that governments tend to learn (or borrow) from countries with similar ideological outlooks. Lumby and Foskett make a similar point, from a different analytical perspective, when they describe the tendency for policy-makers to use defensive and self-referential reasoning to defend their 'espoused theories'. Rational criticism in the spirit of our normative model of policy learning may merely reinforce this behaviour and strengthen existing ideologies. The policy community needs to be prepared to engage with evidence that may be uncomfortable.

Third, there is a need for longer timescales or, at least, for a recognition that policy-making schedules should reflect the needs of policy learning as well as political and administrative imperatives. Time and again the chapters in this book have pointed to the limitations on policy learning arising from compressed policy timescales. Effective policy learning requires time to develop mutual understanding and trust, time to develop learning partnerships, time to accumulate policy memory, time to identify and assemble relevant evidence and time to deliberate and to learn. A government which claims to believe in evidence-informed policy but does not adjust its policy timescales accordingly should not be taken at its word.

Finally, a learning culture needs to be based on – and to celebrate – diversity and collaboration with other participants in the research process who can bring different sorts of policy knowledge to the table. This brings us to the fourth and final area for improvement.

Governance arrangements to promote policy learning

In the end, it is a question of power. Several chapters describe how policy learning may be encouraged or impeded by systems of governance. A common theme is that systems with very unequal power relationships, especially between government and practitioners, are unlikely to provide an effective basis for policy learning. In such systems performance management and accountability frameworks distort and select the information that is fed back to policy-makers at the centre (Spours, Hodgson and Yeomans; Hodgson and Spours). Learning tends to be filtered on ideological grounds. Challenging information and ideas are blocked in precisely those policy-making contexts – the context of practice rather than of influence or text production – where the prevailing ideologies most need to be tested against current experience (Raffe and Spours; Spours, Hodgson and Yeomans). Learning between the home countries has also been affected by unequal power relations; since devolution made these relations a little more equal, mutual learning has been less obstructed by identity politics and the need to protect areas of autonomy (Raffe).

Effective policy learning is ultimately tied to democratic issues –

broadening the scope of those involved in the learning process and ensuring that power is properly distributed to the levels within the system where decision-making can be more properly made. In Chapter 1 we discussed the relationship between politics and policy learning. We identified a rationalist model of governance in which a technocratic concept of policy learning was separate from politics, and a politicised model in which policy learning was subordinated to the ruling political ideology or project. We argued that effective policy learning was most likely to occur in a third model, the collaborative, where it was integrated with politics. We believe that the evidence of the various chapters in this book supports this conclusion. We need to move from a position which acknowledges the limitations of top-down policy to one which actively recognises the virtues of collaboration and deliberation.

Governments in all three countries – England, Scotland and Wales – recognise the importance of practitioners contributing to more effective 14–19 and upper secondary arrangements. However, this is not yet part of a more comprehensive strategy to improve policy learning. Practitioner involvement without wider changes in governance can only serve to 'correct' existing policy. A central point that comes through the chapters, albeit in their different ways, is that the long-standing problems affecting 14–19 education in England and the realisation of implementation strategies in Scotland and Wales, will require a far more participative and deliberative approach to policy-making and policy learning that can generate new solutions.

References

Croxford, L. (2006) *The Youth Cohort Surveys – How good is the evidence?* Special Centre for Educational Sociology (CES) Briefing No. 38. Edinburgh: CES, University of Edinburgh.

Department for Education and Skills (DfES) (2005) *The 14–19 Implementation Plan*. London: DfES.

Olsen, J.P. and Peters, B.G. (1996) *Lessons from Experience: Experiential learning in administrative reforms in eight democracies*. Oslo: Scandinavian University Press.

Index